Digital Design
with
Verilog® HDL

Eliezer Sternheim Ph.D.
Interpretive Systems

Rajvir Singh
Nexgen Microsystems

Yatin Trivedi
Sun Microsystems

Design Automation Series

Automata Publishing Company, Cupertino, CA 95014

Cover design: Sam Starfas
Interior design: Kate Rushford Murray
Printed by: Technical Printers, Inc., Santa Clara

 Copyright ©1990 by Interpretive Systems

Published by Automata Publishing Company

For additional copies of this book or for the source code
to the examples, see the order form on the last page of the
book.

Automata Publishing Company
10487 Westacres Dr., Cupertino CA 95014
Phone: 408-255-0705 Fax: 415-855-9545

Printed in the United States of America
10 9 8 7 6 5 4 3 2

ISBN 0-9627488-0-3

*To
our families
and friends
who make this,
and all things,
possible.*

Foreword

For large systems, gate-level design is dead. For over 25 years, logic schematics served as the *lingua franca* of logic design. Not any more. Today, hardware complexity has outrun schematics with chips so complex that schematics show only a web of connectivity, not the functionality of the design. Engineers are therefore moving toward hardware description languages (HDLs). The most prominent modern hardware description languages are Verilog and VHDL.

This book is the first text to directly address high level HDL-based design. It is a designer's book, not a tedious text. With a quick and useful introduction to the language, it steps right off into design with the how, not just the what, of an HDL. Its authors are real-life designers who saw a better way to teach people HDL-based design.

Here you will see just how you can use an HDL to describe a design, a real design, not just trivial examples. Included are a simple 32-bit pipelined computer, a cache memory design, a UART, and a floppy disk subsystem. In a little over 200 pages, you can get a good start on HDL-based design. Even better, this book is extremely well laid out, easy to understand, and fun to read—like a good design.

Verilog is an HDL created in 1985 by Gateway (later merged with Cadence). Currently, Verilog is the top HDL, used by over 10,000 designers at a wide range of hardware vendors and system houses, including Sun Microsystems, Apple Computer, Nexgen Microsystems, Motorola (for the 68040), and Stardent. Designers like Verilog. It works.

HDLs, coupled with logic synthesis, are the stuff of the future. Here in a simple and straightforward presentation, you can see how to use it. This book is probably one of the best investments a designer can make. Good luck.

Ray Weiss
Senior Technology Editor
E.E. Times

Preface

As electronic designs get larger and more complex, gate-level descriptions become unmanageable and incomprehensible, making it necessary to express designs in more abstract ways. Just as in the 1970s, when high level programming languages replaced assembly languages, in the 1990s, hardware description languages (HDLs) will replace gate-level schematics. Logic synthesis tools will perform the gate-level implementation. Incorporating an HDL and a synthesizer into design methods will no longer be an option but a necessity.

At present, there are two dominant hardware description languages, Verilog and VHDL. Both are public domain languages and have become standards for digital design. The Verilog HDL provides a very concise and readable syntax. Many large pieces of hardware have been designed with Verilog.

Synopsis

With increasing usage of Verilog for system and VLSI design, we saw the usefulness of a text which could help designers in writing Verilog models. Many more designers, who are either using some other HDLs or schematic editors, or are new to the field of hardware design, may want to learn about Verilog in particular and top-down design methods in general.

This book is the outcome of real-world experience with Verilog. Our intent is to show how to functionally describe pieces of hardware in Verilog using a top-down design approach. This design method is illustrated by taking large system examples. All the models presented here have been simulated and verified using the Verilog-XL 1.5 simulator.

i

We expect our readers to have a background in logic design. Some experience in programming in a high-level language, such as C or any other hardware description language, will certainly help. Models in the text are stripped down to retain simplicity for ease of understanding. However, these models can be extended to incorporate the full functionality of the corresponding design.

Although Verilog provides language constructs for designing at lower levels, namely gate and switch levels, such details are not covered in this text. They are fully covered in the Verilog language reference manual obtainable from Cadence Design Systems.

We hope that our readers will find this text useful in designing large systems and complex VLSI devices with Verilog HDL. This text should help stimulate growth in the trend of designing with hardware description languages as opposed to schematics. The concept of top-down design illustrated here for Verilog should be applicable to any other language.

Organization of the Book

The book is organized to present material in a progressive manner. It begins with an introduction to the Verilog HDL and ends with a complete example of modeling and testing a large subsystem. In between it presents modeling concepts of various pieces of hardware: instruction set model of a computer, pipelined CPU control, datapath elements, RAM, CAM, caches, clocks, and asynchronous input/output.

Chapter 2, although a good summary of the language, concentrates mainly on the behavior modeling constructs of Verilog. An example is given to illustrate the top-down design method by mixing behavioral descriptions of low-level blocks with structural descriptions of high-level topology.

Chapter 3 introduces a 32-bit small instruction set computer, SISC, and describes how to model a VLSI processor at the architecture and register transfer levels. It explains the problem of register interlocks and provides a model for a solution to the problem. Concepts of pipelined control are explained and the corresponding Verilog model is presented for a three-stage pipeline.

Chapter 4 goes one step further and shows how to model various building blocks of the SISC and its CPU. It takes the architectural description of Chapter 3 and comes up with a top-level structural description of the SISC system. Subsequent sections present functional models for the datapath, control unit, memories, and clocks.

Chapter 5 discusses cache memories and presents a model of a cache subsystem. Various architectural alternatives for improving the performance of the model are described.

Chapter 6 discuses modeling an asynchronous input/output device. A dual UART is used as an example. The chapter begins with a structural model of the dual UART and goes on to develop a functional model of the single UART module. A model is presented to provide a scheme for testing the dual UART.

Chapter 7 presents a complete example of modeling a large device. It takes a floppy disk subsystem and builds models for its controller and disk drive units. A test module is included to test the subsystem. This chapter is a good illustration for the top-down design method and is applicable to any large or small system.

Chapter 8 provides some useful tips and techniques for modeling and debugging. It shows how to model bidirectional ports, bus transactions in pipelined environment, large memories, loading of interleaved memories, etc.

We have included the full listing of models for all the examples at the end of each chapter.

Acknowledgements

This book has benefited by contributions from Sudhi Balakrisna and Warren Stapleton of Nexgen Microsystems; Sudhi and Warren contributed the chapters on Modeling System Blocks and Cache Memories, respectively. Both were intimately involved in the final reviews of the book. We received invaluable help from our colleagues at Nexgen Microsystems; we want to thank Shrenik Mehta, Bill Fisher, Dave Roth, Dan Curran, and Teresa Butzerin for reviewing various parts of this manuscript, and Dave Stiles for helping us make the initial table of contents.

We are deeply indebted to Atiq Raza and Thampy Thomas of Nexgen Microsystems, for providing us with the system resources which we used for text preparation and model simulation. They encouraged us throughout the project.

We sincerely acknowledge the guidance we received from various groups of Cadence Design Systems, Inc. in Boston and San Jose. Martha Cover and Ed Haas spent numerous hours working through late nights and weekends to review and edit the final manuscript. Sam Starfas designed and prepared the artwork for the book cover. Amy Witherow arranged all the help we needed to prepare the camera ready copy for printing.

We want to thank the following people who critiqued various aspects of the book during its preparation: Suhas Patil of Cirrus Logic, Inc., Avtar Saini and Deepak Verma of Intel Corporation, Steve Thomas and Hal Broome of Intergraph Corporation, Jay Sethuram of NEC Technologies, Inc., Len Shar and B. Kumar of Panasys Corporation, Maqsoodul Mannan of National Semiconductor Corporation, David Hiromoto of Amdahl Corporation, Hamid Butt of Compaq Computer Corporation, Chetan Saiya and Somayazulu Pullela of Tandem Corporation, Kevin Christiansen of Apple Computer, Inc., Arun Biyani of Via Technology, Inc., and Waqar Shah of Advanced Micro Devices. Many of their ideas have made their ways into this manuscript. We also want to thank Kate Murray for the interior design of the book and for final completion of the text in FrameMaker on Apple's Macintosh.

Eli Sternheim
Raj Singh
Yatin Trivedi

June 1990

T A B L E

O F

C O N T E N T S

C H A P T E R

1

Why Hardware Description Languages?

Evolutionary Trends in Design Methods

The use of hardware description languages (HDLs) for logic design has greatly expanded in the last few years. Engineering managers no longer face the dilemma of whether to design with an HDL or not.

Instead, their concern is for selecting a language and incorporating it into their design environment. Designers now prefer to express their design in a functional or behavioral form, deferring the details of implementation to a later stage in the design. An abstract representation helps designers explore architectural alternatives and to detect design bottlenecks before detailed design begins.

There are several reasons for the wide acceptability of HDLs over the traditional—and slowly disappearing—way of designing with schematics.

As a result of vastly improved technologies, both chip density and design complexity are steadily increasing. Densities of more than a million transistors on a chip can be attained, and to make such complexity comprehensible to the human mind, it is necessary to express the functionality in a high level language that hides the details of implementation. This is also why high level programming languages replaced assembly languages in large system programs.

The electronics field is becoming more and more competitive. New entrants to the market are generating tremendous pressure to increase efficiency of logic design, to reduce design cost, and most important, to reduce time to market. Extensive simulation can detect design errors before the chip is manufactured, thus reducing the number of design iterations. An efficient HDL and the host simulation system have become invaluable in minimizing the number of design errors and have made it possible to have functional chips in the first silicon.

The trend toward larger and more complex designs will continue. In the 1990s we will see designs approaching the million-gate count. Engineers will inevitably design with an HDL and leave the implementation to logic synthesis tools.

Designing with HDLs

Expressing designs in a hardware description language (HDL) can provide several benefits. An HDL description can be used as a specification of the design. The advantage of using a formal language, such as Verilog® HDL, to specify a design is that the specification is complete and unambiguous. Formal language specification is "soft" compared to the "hard" form of schematics. An HDL representation allows for easy text processing on any word processor or design-specific tools, whereas binary schematics databases usually require a graphics editor or vendor-specific tools.

A second purpose of using an HDL is simulation. Simulating the design can uncover errors that would otherwise be detected only when the hardware is built. Simulation can be performed at several levels. At the functional level, the system is described using high level constructs. At the logic level, the system is described hierarchically where at the bottom of the hierarchy are the basic building blocks. This level can include timing delay information, allowing for timing analysis, whereby setup/hold time can be checked and verified.

A third purpose for using HDL is logic synthesis. There are synthesis tools which can take an HDL description of a design and generate a gate-level implementation with library components. These tools optimize the design with respect to speed, circuit size, or some other cost function. Existing synthesis tools have some limitations; for example, they use only a subset of the language, and the synthesized circuit may not be as efficient as if it were implemented by an expert designer. Still, synthesizing even a portion of the design can save both time and money, and allows for easy prototyping and initial speed/area estimates.

Finally, HDL is the best way to document a design. A well commented HDL description can give better and more concise documentation than a set of schematics that show gate level details.

Designing with Verilog HDL

Verilog HDL is simple and elegant. It provides constructs to describe hardware elements in a succinct and readable form. A comparable description, for example in VHDL, can be twice as long as a Verilog description.

In Verilog, a designer needs to learn only one language for all aspects of logic design. Simulation of a design, at least, requires functional models, hierarchical structures, test vectors, and man/machine interaction. In Verilog, all of these are achieved by one language. Almost every statement that can be written in procedural code can also be issued in an interactive session from the terminal.

Verilog is not only concise and uniform, but also is easy to learn. It is very similar to the C programming language. Since C is one of the most widely used programming languages, most designers should be familiar with it and may, therefore, find it easy to learn Verilog.

2

Anatomy of the Verilog HDL

In this chapter we introduce briefly the Verilog hardware description language. We do not intend to provide a complete summary of the language. A full description of Verilog HDL is available in the language reference manual. This chapter, and the book in general, concentrates mainly on the behavioral aspects of the language. Appendix A gives the Verilog syntax and Appendix B gives a list of Verilog keywords.

In this book the term Verilog refers to the Verilog hardware description language, as opposed to the Verilog-XL simulator. All keywords prefixed by '$' sign are Verilog-XL system commands and are not part of the Verilog language.

Verilog bears close resemblance to the C programming language. Designers with exposure to C will find it easy to learn and use Verilog. Like C, Verilog is a free format, case sensitive language, with all the keywords in lower case. Spaces, tabs, new lines and comments can be used to improve readability.

The Concept of a Module

A module is the basic unit in Verilog. It represents some logical entity that is usually implemented in a piece of hardware. For example, a module can be a simple gate, a 32-bit counter, a memory subsystem, a computer system, or a network of computers.

Before we get into details of the language constructs, let us look at an example of a module definition (Figure 2.1).

```
module add2bit (in1, in2, sum);
input in1, in2;
output[1:0] sum;
wire in1, in2;
reg[1:0] sum;

always @(in1 or in2) begin
   sum = in1 + in2;
   $display ("The sum of %b and %b is %0d (time = %0d)",
   in1, in2, sum, $time);
end

endmodule
```

Figure 2.1 A module definition example

The add2bit module in the example has two inputs and one output. The inputs are one bit each and are declared as wires. The output is declared as a two bit wide register. The module has one executable block placed between the statement "always ... begin" and "end". It continuously monitors its inputs, and when one of the inputs changes, the module calculates the output as the sum of the two inputs and prints the values of the inputs, the output and the current simulation time.

Although add2bit is a very simple module, it does demonstrate the main components that all modules have. Figure 2.2 shows the syntax of module definition.

Each module has a header which contains the module name and the list of inputs and outputs. This describes the means by which a module interacts with its environment. All the (external) inputs and outputs as well as the (internal) variables have to be declared. Typically they are declared as either wires, which simply provide interconnections among the subunits of the module, or registers which can hold state

```
module <module_name> <optional list of input/outputs> ;
<input/output declarations>
<local variable declarations>

<module_item>
...
<module_item>

endmodule
```

Figure 2.2 Module definition syntax

information and whose value can be modified using behavioral statements.

The core of the module body in Figure 2.3 is represented by <module_items>. These items can be of several different types, the most common of which are continuous assignments, structural instances and behavioral instances.

A continuous assignment is a compact way for describing a combinational section of the module. For example, the lines:

```
wire[7:0] result;
assign result = op1 + op2;
```

or the equivalent line:

```
wire[7:0] result = op1 + op2;
```

both define result as the sum of op1 and op2. Whenever op1 or op2 changes, result is recalculated.

A structural instance is an instance of a lower level module in the current one. For example the lines

```
fulladd f1 (cin0, a0, b0, sum0, cout0);
fulladd f2 (cout0, a1, b1, sum1, cout2);
```

instantiate two fulladd modules in the current module, and give them the names f1 and f2. Structural instantiation is equivalent to embedding a lower level schematic in the current one. If a module consists of only structural instances, then the module is a netlist representation.

Since structural instances only define the partition and the hierarchy of the module, there must be a way to define the functionality of the bottom level modules. One way to define functionality is to use the Verilog primitives, such as AND gates, OR gates, etc. But although gate

7

level designs can be made very efficient, the preferred way, and the one that Verilog encourages, is to use higher level behavioral constructs to define the model functionality, namely behavioral instances.

A behavioral instance is a block of Verilog code that is preceded by the keyword "initial" or "always". All the instances in a module (both behavioral and structural) execute concurrently. An "initial" behavioral instance executes its code once at the beginning of the simulation. For example the block:

```
initial
    i = 0;
```

initializes i to 0 at the beginning of the simulation. An "always" behavioral instance executes its code continuously in an infinite loop. For example the block:

```
always
    #10 i = i + 1;
```

increments i by 1 every 10 time units throughout the simulation.

The rest of this chapter provides a summary of the behavioral aspect of Verilog.

Basic Data Types

Like most programming languages, Verilog supports constants which hold fixed data and variables which can be modified during simulation. Constants in Verilog can be decimal, hexadecimal, octal or binary, and have the format

```
width'radix value
```

where width is an optional decimal integer describing the width of the constant, radix is optional and can be one of b, B, d, D, o, O, h, and H.

```
B and b indicate a binary constant,
O and o indicate an octal constant,
D and d indicate a decimal constant, and
H and h indicate a hexadecimal constant.
```

Radix B and b indicate a binary constant, radix O and o indicate an octal constant, radix D and d indicate a decimal constant, and radix H and h indicate a hexadecimal constant.

If width is not specified, then it is inferred from the value of the constant, and if radix is not specified then a decimal radix is assumed. Some examples are:

```
15              (decimal 15)
'h15            (decimal 21, hex 15)
5'b10011        (decimal 19, binary 10011)
12'h01F         (decimal 31, hex 01F)
```

String constants are written between two double quotes (e.g., "mystring") and are converted to their ASCII equivalent binary format. For example, the string "ab" is equivalent to 16'h5758.

Variables in Verilog can be of type reg (register), wire, integer, real, event, and time. Whereas the integer, float, time and event types represent abstract concepts, the reg and wire types can be directly mapped to hardware. Wires represent interconnections among units, and registers represent memory elements. Both registers and wires have a width, specified at declaration, or defaulted to 1. Each bit in a register or a wire variable can take one of the four values: 1, 0, x, and z. An x represents either an uninitialized variable, or a conflict, such as when two outputs are tied together and each tries to drive the signal to a different value. A z represents high impedance or a floating value and is used for tristate buses. Register and wires can be used in arithmetic expressions and are interpreted by the simulator as unsigned integers.

Here are some examples of declarations of variables:

```
integer  i, j;            // two integers
real  f, d;               // two real numbers
wire [7:0] bus            // 8-bits wide bus
reg [0:15] word;          // 16-bits wide word
event  trigger,clock_high; // two events
time  t_setup,t_hold;     // t1, t2
```

Single- and multi-bit subfields of registers and wires are treated like other variables and can be accessed and modified in expressions:

```
reg [15:0] word;
reg [7:0] byte;
...
word[0] = ...             // The rightmost bit of word
byte = ...+word[15:8];    // The left half of word
... word ...              // Equivalent to word[15:0]
```

The following examples illustrate variable usage in Verilog expressions:

```
i = i + j;
assign  bus = word[15:8] + word[7:0];
f = (g + 1.2) * 3.29E-5;
@e1 #5 ->e2; // wait for event e1 to be triggered,
             // wait for 5 time units
             // and trigger event e2
if ($time - t1 < t2) error ("timing violations");
```

Integers are 32 bit signed numbers that can hold temporary variables. Time variables can hold simulation time values, and are implemented usually as 64 bit unsigned integers. Event and time variables will be discussed later in "The concept of time and events" section.

Verilog has only one data structure, namely the array which can be of any variable type. Following are some examples of array declarations:

```
integer num[99:0];     // array of 100 integers
reg [7:0]mem[0:1024];  // array of 1024 bytes
reg [10*8:1]names[20]; // array of 20 names,
                       // each name is 10 char long
                       // each char is an 8-bit byte
```

Accessing an array item has the same syntax as accessing a bit in a vector, thus word[i] can be the i'th item in the array word, or the i'th bit in the vector word, depending on how word was declared. To access a bit subfield of an array element, the element has to be stored first in a temporary variable:

```
reg [15:0] array [0:10];
reg [15:0] temp;
...
temp = array[3];
... temp[7:5] ...
```

Basic Operators and Expressions

The Verilog language borrows syntax and semantics of most of its operations from the C programming language. A notable exception is the absence of autoincrement (++) and autodecrement (--) operators. Figure 2.3 gives a summary of Verilog's operators. Figure 2.6 gives the operator precedence.

```
+    -   *   /            (arithmetic)
>   >=   <   <=           (relational)
!   &&   ||               (logical)
==   !=                   (logical equality)
?:                        (conditional)
{}                        (concatenate)
%                         (modulus)
===   !==                 (case equality)
~    &   |                (bit-wise)
<<   >>                   (shift)
```

Figure 2.3 Summary of language operators

All the binary operators can also be used as unary reduction operators. For example, the expression "+varname" will return the sum of all the bits of varname. A more typical example of reduction usage is "^varname" which is the exclusive "or" of all the bits of varname, producing its parity. Other examples of the unary reduction operators are the expression

```
^word === 'bx // True if any bit in word is x
```

or the expression

```
&word == 0 // True if any bit in word is 0
```

The logical comparison operators are also identical to those of C. When comparing two variables that are not 0 or 1 (i.e. ,x or z) the equivalence operator always returns false. To check the equivalence of variables which may contain x or z, Verilog provides the comparison operators "===" and "!==". Figure 2.4 shows the difference between "==" and "===".

```
module equ_equ;

  initial begin
    $display ("'bx == 'bx is %b", 'bx == 'bx);
    $display ("'bx === 'bx is %b", 'bx === 'bx);
    $display ("'bz != 'bx is %b", 'bz != 'bx);
    $display ("'bz !== 'bx is %b", 'bz !== 'bx);
  end

endmodule
```

Figure 2.4 Difference between "==" and "==="

Execution of the module equ_equ will produce the following results:

```
'bx == 'bx is x
'bx === 'bx is 1
'bz != 'bx is x
'bz !== 'bx is 1
```

Two operators that are not in C, are the concatenation and the replication operators. Two or more variables (or constants) can be concatenated by enclosing them in curly braces ({}), separated by commas:

```
{2'b1x, 4'h7} === 6'b1x0111
```

Concatenated variables can appear in any expression, or they can appear on the left hand side of an assignment operator. A constant that appears in a concatenation, has to have explicit width (e.g., 1'bz rather than 'bz). The size of the concatenation is the sum of the sizes of its constituents.

Replication provides a short form notation for duplicating a constant or a variable. An expression can be replicated by enclosing it in two sets of curly braces and providing the replication factor between the first two opening braces:

```
{3{2'b01}} === 6'b010101
```

Figure 2.5 shows an example of using concatenation to swap two bytes, and using replication to do sign extension of a word.

Expressions can be combined using the normal precedence rules (Figure 2.6). Parenthesis can be used to improve the readability and avoid ambiguities

Procedural Statements

While expressions can be used to calculate a value, they cannot be evaluated in isolation, but have to be part of a statement. A simple statement can be an assignment statement or it can be a control flow statement. A compound statement, or a block, consists of a group of statements enclosed within "begin" and "end". Every behavioral instance

```
module concat_replicate(swap,signextend);

  input swap,signextend;

  reg[15:0] word;
  reg[31:0] double;
  reg[ 7:0] byte1, byte2;

  initial begin
    byte1 = 5; byte2 = 7;
    if (swap)
      word = {byte2, byte1};
    else
      word = {byte1, byte2};
    if (signextend)
      double = {{16{word[15]}},word};
    else
      double = word;
  end

endmodule
```

(handwritten annotations: concat; concat; replicate bit 15; concat)

Figure 2.5 Concatenation and replication

is composed of a simple or a compound statement. A block may be named:

```
begin : instruction_fetch
...
end
```

where the identifier following the ":" is the block name. Named blocks can have local variables declared in them.

```
* / %              Highest precedence
+ -
<< >>
< <= > >=
== !== === !==
&
^ ^~
|
&&                 Lowest precedence
```

Figure 2.6 Operator Precedence

```
module for_loop;

  integer i;

  initial
    for (i = 0; i < 4; i = i + 1) begin
    $display ("i = %0d (%b binary)", i, i);
  end

endmodule
```

Figure 2.7 A for loop statement

The Verilog language contains many of the control constructs of other high level languages, and of C in particular.

The for Loop

The following example (Figure 2.7) shows the use of a for loop.

Execution of the for_loop module produces the following results:
```
i = 0 (0 binary)
i = 1 (1 binary)
i = 2 (10 binary)
i = 3 (11 binary)
```

The while Loop

The effect of the for loop can also be attained using a while construct as shown in Figure 2.8. Execution of the while loop module produces the same results as produced by the for loop module in Figure 2.7.

```
module while_loop;

  integer i;

  initial begin
    i = 0;
    while (i < 4) begin
      $display ("i = %d (%b binary)", i, i);
      i = i + 1;
    end
  end

endmodule
```

Figure 2.8 A while loop statement

```
module case_statement;

   integer i;

   intitial i = 0;

   always begin
     $display ("i = %0d", i);
     case (i)
       0: i = i + 2;
       1: i = i + 7;
       2: i = i - 1;
       default: $stop;
     endcase
   end

endmodule
```

Figure 2.9 A case statement

The case Statement

The following example (Figure 2.9) shows the use of the case control structure. The case statement corresponds to the switch statement in C.

Execution of the case statement module produces the following results:

```
i =  0
i =  2
i =  1
i =  8
```

The selection expression is compared against the case expressions, and the match is done on a bit by bit basis (similar to the operator ===). If none of the cases match, then the default case will be executed. If no default case exists, then the execution continues after the case statement. It is a good programming practice to always provide a default clause in a case statement. If such a case can not occur, then the model may be programmed to print an error message or stop the simulation.

The casez and casex statements are very similar to the case statement with one exception. The casez statement handles z bits as don't care, while the casex statement handles both z and x bits as don't care.

```
module repeat_loop (clock);
  input clock;

  initial begin
    repeat (5)
      @(posedge clock);
      $stop;
    end

endmodule
```

Figure 2.10 A repeat loop

The repeat Loop

Verilog has two more control structures which are not very common in other programming languages, the repeat and the forever constructs. Figure 2.10 describes a repeat loop which waits for 5 clock cycles and then stops the simulation.

The forever Loop

Figure 2.11 shows a forever loop, which monitors some condition and displays a message when the condition occurs.

Even though both the repeat and the forever statements can be implemented using other control statements, e.g. the for statement, they are very convenient especially in issuing commands interactively from

```
module forever_statement(a,b,c);

  input a,b,c;

    initial forever begin
      @(a or b or c)
      if (a + b == c) begin
        $display ("a(%d)+b(%d) = c(%d)",a,b,c);
        $stop;
      end
    end

endmodule
```

Figure 2.11 A forever loop

the keyboard. They have the advantage of not requiring any variables to be declared a priori.

The Concept of Time and Events

So far, describing behavior in Verilog is more like programming in any structured high level language. The single most important difference between the two is the concept of time, and its effect on the execution order of statements in a module. In most programming language, there is a single program counter which indicates the current location of program execution. Since in hardware all the elements operate in parallel, a serial model for execution is not appropriate in an HDL, and therefore, in Verilog execution is event driven. A global variable designates the simulation time. At each point in time there may be one or more events scheduled to be executed. The event scheduler of the Verilog simulator takes the place of the program counter of a prgramming language

The Verilog simulator executes all the events scheduled for the current simulation time and removes them from the event list. When no more events exist for the current simulation time, then the simulation time advances to the first element scheduled for the next time. As events are being executed, new events are usually being generated for a future time (or possibly for the current time).

Figure 2.12 depicts the simulation time axis with several events scheduled at different points. Note that the time before the current simulation time can not have any events associated with it, since all the events have been executed and removed.

The order of event execution within the same simulation time, in general, is not known, and one cannot rely on it, since the Verilog simulator may try to optimize execution by ordering the events in a particular way. However, Verilog ensures that a linear code which does not have any timing control will execute as a single event without interruption. Also, the order of execution between any two identical simulation runs will also be identical. The example of Figure 2.13 illustrates this point by using multiple behavioral instances.

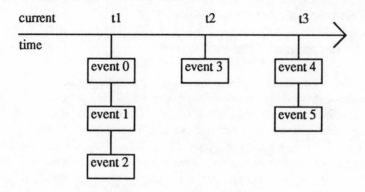

Figure 2.12 The axis of time

```
module event_control;

  register [4:0] r;

  initial begin
    $display ("First initial block, line 1.");
    $display ("First initial block, line 2.");
  end

  initial
    for (r = 0; r <= 3; r = r + 1)
      $display ("r = %0b", r);

endmodule
```

execute @
same time

Figure 2.13 Multiple behavioral instances

Execution of the event_control module produces the following results:

```
First initial block, line 1.
First initial block, line 2.
r = 0
r = 1
r = 10
r = 11
```

Here, All the initial blocks are scheduled to execute at the same simulation time (time 0).

Referring to simulation results of Figure 2.13, one can see that Verilog chose some order of execution of the blocks which is not obvious from the code of the model. But note that once a block has been scheduled for execution, it continues to execute until completion.

Time and Event Control

A Verilog process (i.e. an initial or always block) can reschedule its own execution by using one of the three time control forms:

```
#expression
@event-expression
wait (expression)
```

The #expression form, used for synchronous control, suspends the execution of the process for a fixed time period specified by "time", while the @event-expression form, used for asynchronous control, suspends the execution until the specified event occurs. In both cases the scheduler removes the currently executing events from the events list of the current simulation time and puts it on some future events list.

The wait expression form is a level sensitive event control. If the wait expression is false, execution will be suspended until it becomes true (through the execution of some statement in another process).

The example of Figure 2.14 shows the use of time control structure.

Execution of the time_control module produces the following results:

```
r = 2 at time 5
r = 1 at time 10
r = 2 at time 25
r = 1 at time 30
r = 2 at time 55
r = 1 at time 60
```

Note the first initial statement

```
initial #70 $stop;
```

which is a common way to limit the simulation run to a fixed time.

```
module time_control;

   reg[1:0] r;

   initial #70 $stop;

   initial begin : b1 // Note a named block, b1
      #10  r = 1; // wait for 10 time units
      #20  r = 1; // wait for 20 time units
      #30  r = 1; // wait for 30 time units
   end

   initial begin : b2 // Note a named block, b2
      #5   r = 2; // wait for 5 time units
      #20  r = 2; // wait for 20 time units
      #30  r = 2; // wait for 30 time units
   end

   always @r begin
      $display ("r = %0d at time %0d", r, $time);
   end

endmodule
```

Figure 2.14 Example of time control

In this example, even though all the initial blocks started at the same time, some of them were suspended (and rescheduled) at different points on the simulation time. Note the use of named blocks (b1 and b2). A named block can have local variables declared in it, although this example did not exploit this property and used the names as a notation convenience only.

The @event-expression form of control, waits for an event to occur before continuing the execution of the block. An event can be one of several forms:

```
(a)  variable <or variable> ....
(b)  posedge one-bit-variable
(c)  negedge one-bit-variable
(d)  event-variable
```

In form (a), execution is delayed until any of the variables has changed. In form (b) and (c) execution is delayed until the variable has changed from 0, x, or z to 1 (if posedge) or from 1, x, or z to 0 (if negedge). In form (d), execution of the block is suspended until the event is triggered.

20

```
module event_control;

  event e1, e2;

  initial @e1 begin
    $display ("I am in the middle.");
    ->e2;
  end

 initial @e2
    $display ("I am supposed to execute last.");

  initial begin
    $display ("I am the first.");
    ->e1;
  end

endmodule
```

Figure 2.15 Example of event control

An event can be triggered by executing the expression ->event-variable. The following example of Figure 2.15 uses event variables to control the order of execution of three initial blocks which execute at the same simulation time.

Execution of the module event_control will produce the following results:

```
I am the first.
I am in the middle.
I am supposed to execute last.
```

This form of control ensures the order of execution. Without the event control statement, the Verilog scheduler can choose to schedule the "initial" blocks in any arbitrary order.

A special form of the time and event control construct is their use inside an assignment statement. The assignment

```
current_state = #clock_period next_state;
```

is equivalent to the following two statements

```
temp = next_state;
#clock_period current_state = next_state;
```

and similarly, the assignment

```
current_state = @(posedge clock) next_state;
```

is equivalent to the two statements

```
temp = next_state;
@(posedge clock) current_state = temp;
```

The Concept of Parallelism

Verilog has a few other control structures which are not common in other programming languages. One is the fork-join construct, and the other is the disable statement.

The fork-join Pair

Figure 2.16 shows an example of the use of the fork-join construct.

```
module fork_join;

  event a, b;

    initial
      fork
        @a ;
        @b ;         } both
      join
    end

endmodule
```

Figure 2.16 Example of parallel processes

In this example, execution of the initial block will be suspended until both events, a and b, are triggered in some order. During the fork, two or more execution threads are activated. When all of them are complete, execution continues at the join. If some of the threads finish before the others, these threads suspend and wait for the rest.

The disable Statement

The disable statement works like the break statement of C. But whereas the break statement in a C program only modifies the program counter, the disable statement has to remove pending events from the events queues. The disable takes as argument a block name and removes

```
module disable_block;

  event a, b;

  // Block name is needed
  initial begin : block1
    fork
      @a disable block1;
      @b disable block1;
    join
  end

endmodule
```

either

Figure 2.17 Example of disable

the rest of the events associated with this block from the queue. Only named blocks or tasks can be disabled.

The following example of Figure 2.17 is a modification of the previous one, but instead of waiting for both the events a and b to occur, this module waits only for one of them, either a or b to occur.

Functions and Tasks

One of the most powerful modeling techniques in Verilog is the encapsulation of a piece of code in a task or a function. Figure 2.19 shows an example of a task.

```
function [7:0] func;

  input   i1;
  integer i1;

  reg [7:0] rg;

  begin
    rg = 1;
    for (i = 1; i <= i1; i++)
      rg = rg+1;
    func = rg;
  end

endfuction
```

Figure 2.18 Example of a function

23

```
task tsk;

  input i1, i2;
  output o1, o2;

    $display("Task tsk, i1=%0b, i2=%0b",i1,i2);
    #1 o1 = i1 & i2;
    #1 o2 = i1 | i2;

endtask
```

Figure 2.19 Example of a task

There are a few differences between a task and a function.

A task may have timing control constructs, whereas a function may not. This means that a function executes in zero simulation time and returns immediately (it is essentially combinational), whereas a task may have delays, and the code that initiated the task has to wait until the task completes execution or until the task is disabled, before continuing the execution. The execution control returns to the statement immediately following the one which initiated the task or the function.

A task may have both inputs and outputs, whereas a function must have at least one input and does not have any output. A function returns its results by its name.

A task invocation is a statement, whereas a function is invoked when it is referenced in an expression. For example:

```
    tsk (out, in1, in2);
```
invokes a task, named tsk, and
```
    i = func (a, b, c);  // or
    assign x = func (y);
```
invokes a function, named func.

Figure 2.18 shows an example of a function.

Functions play an important role in logic synthesis. Since functions are combinational, they are also synthesizeable, and can be used in describing the system. Tasks are a very important tool in organizing the code and making it readable and maintainable. A piece of code that is used more than once should be encapsulated into a task. This helps to localize any change to this part of the code. If a code is expected to be issued interactively from a terminal, it should also be converted to a task in order to save typing. In addition, it is useful to break long procedural blocks into smaller tasks in order to increase the readability of the code.

The Behavioral Description

Verilog is a top-down design language that supports behavioral description, structural description or a mixed mode description. In the next few sections we will illustrate these aspects of the language with a complete example of a 4-bit adder.

The first example in Figure 2.20 describes the behavior of the 4-bit adder module using high level constructs of Verilog.

Note that the sum and zero ports have been declared as registers. This has been done so that a behavioral statement can assign values to them. This description has two behavioral instances, one an initial instance and one an always instance.

The construct @(in1 or in2) causes the simulation to wait until any of the inputs, in1 or in2, has changed from their last values. Without this

```
module adder4 (in1, in2, sum, zero);

  input   [3:0] in1;
  input   [3:0] in2;
  output  [4:0] sum;
  output  zero;
  reg     [4:0] sum;
  reg     zero;

  initial begin
    sum = 0;
    zero = 1;
  end

  always @(in1 or in2) begin
    sum = in1 + in2;
    if (sum == 0)
      zero = 1;
    else
      zero = 0;
  end

endmodule
```

Figure 2.20 Behavioral description of a 4-bit adder

construct the always loop would compute forever with the same input values and the simulation time will never advance.

Note that an always block can also be programmed as an initial block using a forever control structure as shown in Figure 2.21.

The next example in Figure 2.22 is a modification of the example from Figure 2.20, and it models adder4 using a continuous assignment.

Here, zero is a wire and not a register. Whenever the register sum changes, zero is recalculated using the tertiary operator "? :" which has the same meaning as in the C language and is an expression equivalent to the if-then-else statement. The wire declaration of zero and its

```
initial begin
  forever begin
    @(in1 or in2) begin
      sum = in1 + in2;
      if (sum == 0)
        zero = 1;
      else
        zero = 0;
    end
  end
end
```

Figure 2.21 Using initial-forever instead of always

```
module adder4 (in1, in2, sum, zero);

  input   [3:0] in1;
  input   [3:0] in2;
  output  [4:0] sum;
  reg     [4:0] sum;
  output zero;

  assign zero = (sum == 0) ? 1 : 0;

  initial sum = 0;

  always @(in1 or in2)
    sum = in1 + in2;

endmodule
```

Figure 2.22 Using a continuous assignment

continuous assignment can be combined into a single statement as follows:

```
wire zero = (sum == 0) ? 1 : 0;
```

The Structural Description

The example in Figure 2.23 implements the 4-bit adder module as a structure of 1-bit full adder sub modules and gates.

```
module adder4 (in1, in2, sum, zero);

    input   [3:0] in1;
    input   [3:0] in2;
    output  [4:0] sum;
    output  zero;

    fulladd u1 (in1[0],in2[0], 0,sum[0],c0);
    fulladd u2 (in1[1],in2[1],c0,sum[1],c1);
    fulladd u3 (in1[2],in2[2],c1,sum[2],c2);
    fulladd u4 (in1[3],in2[3],c2,sum[3],sum[4]);

    nor u5 (zero,sum[0],sum[1],sum[2],sum[3],sum[4]);

endmodule
```

Figure 2.23 Structural description of 4-bit adder

In this example, the 4-bit adder is made of four instances of 1-bit adder modules (fulladd) and one instance of nor gate module. This implementation describes the hardware structure and has a one to one correspondence to a schematic. It uses two types of lower level modules: a fulladd and a nor. Even though fulladd is a user defined module and nor is a Verilog primitive, both are instantiated in the same uniform way.

Note that the structural description implicitly declared three wires: c0, c1 and c2. These wires interconnect the carry bit from one fulladd stage to the input of the next fulladd stage. Verilog permits implicit declaration of single bit wires. If the interconnection is a multi bit bus, then an explicit declaration is needed, for example:

```
wire [3:0] databus;
```

Note also that when a module is instantiated, the order of its input/ output ports is important. The higher level module adder4 needs to establish a binding between its nets and the corresponding ports of the lower level module fulladd. Figure 2.24 shows a simple implementation of the fulladd module.

```
module fulladd (in1,in2,carryin,sum,carryout);

   input   in1,in2,carryin;
   output  sum,carryout;

   assign {carryout,sum} = in1 + in2 + carryin;

endmodule
```

Concat?

Figure 2.24 Behavior of a 1-bit full adder

Mixed Mode Representation

The final example in Figure 2.25 describes the adder4 as a combination of structural and behavioral instances.

This model computes the sum output by structural instances of fulladd modules whereas it computes the zero output using a behavioral instance.

```
module adder4 (in1, in2, sum, zero);

   input   [3:0] in1;
   input   [3:0] in2;
   output  [4:0] sum;
   output  zero;
   reg     zero;

   fulladd u1 (in1[0],in2[0], 0,sum[0],c0);
   fulladd u2 (in1[1],in2[1],c0,sum[1],c1);
   fulladd u3 (in1[2],in2[2],c1,sum[2],c2);
   fulladd u4 (in1[3],in2[3],c2,sum[3],sum[4]);

   always @sum
     if (sum == 0)
       zero = 1;
     else
       zero = 0;

endmodule
```

Figure 2.25 Mixed mode representation

C H A P T E R

3

Modeling a Pipelined Processor

In this chapter we take the specification of a 32-bit processor and develop a functional model for it through various stages of successive refinement. First we implement an instruction set model, then we describe a register transfer level (RTL). In the next chapter we arrive at a structural model that maps the processor to various building blocks. In the process, we explain modeling of such concepts as pipeline, concurrency, instruction execution, functional partitioning, and creation of test vectors.

The emphasis here is on the process of modeling as opposed to describing the architecture of a processor. It is not our intention to explain the detailed functionality of any commercial microprocessor or architecture. Some discussion on processor architecture is presented to explain the concepts and process of modeling.

The SISC Processor Example

A typical VLSI processor is specified by its architecture and instruction set. Let us define a Small Instruction Set Computer (SISC) that has only ten instructions: load, store, add, multiply, complement, shift, rotate, nop, halt, and branch. We will design a processor that can execute this SISC instruction set.

Before we discuss the implementation of the processor model, we must understand how it executes programs consisting of a mix of these instructions. That is precisely what we expect to learn from an instruction set model.

A block diagram of the SISC system is shown in Figure 3.1, and the instruction set is described in Figure 3.2.

Instruction Set Model

An instruction set model of a processor describes the effect of executing the instructions and the interactions among them. The

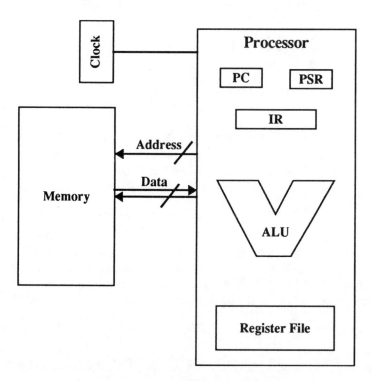

Figure 3.1 Example SISC block diagram

Instructions

Name	Mnemonic	Opcode	Format	(inst dst src)
NOP	NOP	0	NOP	
BRANCH	BRA	1	BRA	mem, cc
LOAD	LD	2	LD	reg, mem1
STORE	STR	3	STR	mem, src
ADD	ADD	4	ADD	reg, src
MULTIPLY	MUL	5	MLT	reg, src
COMPLEMENT	CMP	6	CMP	reg, src
SHIFT	SHF	7	SHF	reg, cnt
ROTATE	ROT	8	ROT	reg, cnt
HALT	HLT	9	HLT	

Condition codes

A	Always	0
C	Carry	1
E	Even	2
P	Parity	3
Z	Zero	4
N	Negative	5

Operand addressing

```
mem  -  Memory address
mem1 -  Memory address or immediate value
reg  -  Any register index
src  -  Any register index, or immediate value
cc   -  condition code
cnt  -  shift/rotate count,>0=right,<0=left,+/-16
```

Instruction format

```
IR[31:28]    Opcode
IR[27:24]    cc
IR[27]       source type 0=reg(mem),1=imm
IR[26]       destination type 0=reg, 1=imm
IR[23:12]    source address
IR[23:12]    shift/rotate count
IR[11:0]     destination address
```

```
Processor status register

PSR[0]   Carry
PSR[1]   Even
PSR[2]   Parity
PSR[3]   Zero
PSR[4]   Negative
```

Figure 3.2 SISC instruction set

implementation of the corresponding hardware to execute these instructions is not the issue. For example, an add instruction may simply be modeled as

```
{carry,sum} = in1 + in2 ;
```

Without going into detail of whether the addition be performed using a ripple-carry adder, a carry-look-ahead adder, or some other algorithm; just that given two inputs (in1 and in2) an addition is performed to produce the sum and the carry.

Similarly, we are not interested in studying or implementing a memory protocol. We treat memory as a large set of registers directly visible to the processor.

The SISC processor model is a "closed system" module without any input or output ports and has the following form:

```
module system ;
        .... // Module items include
        .... // declarations, tasks, functions,
        .... // initial and always blocks, etc.
endmodule  // system
```

In the following sections we describe each of the module items.

Declarations

Since we are modeling at a high level, we should think in terms of registers and register bit-fields rather than gates and switches. Some of the registers we need are

```
32-bit register for holding the instructions
```

```
12-bit register for addressing the memory
5-bit register to hold condition code flags
33-bit register to hold results
```

These and other registers and parameters are declared as shown in Figure 3.3.

The memory and the register file are declared as arrays of registers of size WIDTH. This declaration allows random access to all locations within the memory and the register file, obviating the need for modeling a communication protocol. Access to a memory or a register file location is now a simple matter of referencing the structure with appropriate location as the array index. For example,

```
RFILE[3] = MEM[20] ;
```

will transfer contents of memory location 21 to register file location 4. Notice that we use 0 as the starting index for both the structures.

The size of the maximum addressable memory was derived from the maximum size of the address field, 12-bits. The size of the register file was defined arbitrarily as 16.

```
// Parameter  Declaration

parameter       WIDTH = 32 ;
parameter       CYCLE = 10 ;
parameter       ADDRSIZE = 12 ;
parameter       MAXREGS = 16 ;
parameter       MEMSIZE = (1<<ADDRSIZE);


// Register declarations

reg [WIDTH-1:0]  MEM[0:MEMSIZE-1],
                 RFILE[0:MAXREGS-1],
                 ir, //
                 src1, src2 ;
reg [WIDTH:0]    result ;
reg [ADDRSIZE-1:0]  pc ;
reg [4:0]        psr ;
reg              dir ;
reg              reset ;

integer          i ;
```

Figure 3.3 Declarations for instruction set model

The result register is defined as 33 bits to hold a carry bit after an arithmetic instruction is executed. The program counter, contains the address of an instruction in memory, and therefore has a size of 12. The processor status register, psr, holds the five condition code flags: carry, even, parity, zero, and negative.

The parameter statements declare various symbolic constants such as WIDTH and CYCLE. These symbolic constants allow us to write easily maintainable and customizable models. For example, if the architecture demands 16 kilobytes of memory, we need to change the ADDRSIZE parameter from 12 to 14. This will change the MEMSIZE parameter from 4k to 16k, and declare the memory array mem with its index range from 0 to a maximum of 16k-1.

The 'define statements, shown in Figure 3.4, permit us to refer to various fields of the instruction register and the condition codes by symbolic names rather than by numbers. The use of symbolic names for

```
// Define Instruction fields

'define OPCODE      ir[31:28]
'define SRC         ir[23:12]
'define DST         ir[11:0]
'define SRCTYPE     ir[27]
'define DSTTYPE     ir[26]
'define CCODE       ir[27:24]
'define SRCNT       ir[23:12]

// Operand types

'define REGTYPE     0
'define IMMTYPE     1

// Define opcodes for each instruction

'define NOP     4'b0000
'define BRA     4'b0001
'define LD      4'b0010
'define STR     4'b0011
'define ADD     4'b0100
'define MUL     4'b0101
'define CMP     4'b0110
'define SHF     4'b0111
'define ROT     4'b1000
'define HLT     4'b1001
```

Figure 3.4 Defining symbolic names for bit-fields

various instruction fields in the model description makes the model independent of the arrangement (relative ordering) of these fields in the instruction register. For example, if the order of SRCTYPE and DSTTYPE fields were exchanged, the entire model will need only two lines changed as follows:

```
`define SRCTYPE ir[26]
`define DSTTYPE ir[27]
```

Figure 3.4 shows definitions of symbolic names for bit fields.

The Main Process

One approach to understanding the modeling process is to think of it as a three-step manipulation process. First, identify the basic entities or structures to be manipulated. Next, describe how to manipulate these structures. Finally, verify that the model conforms to the specification.

We defined the entities in the previous section; namely, the registers, the register file, and the memory. Now we describe how to manipulate them.

Without going into the details of the operations of a processor, it suffices to say that a processor continuously performs a "fetch-execute-write" loop. The Verilog description shown in Figure 3.5 models the main process. The main process, described by the always block labeled main_process, is divided into three tasks: fetch, execute, and write_result. The fetch task fetches an instruction from memory, the execute task executes an instruction, and the write_result task writes the result to the register file. This sequence is repeated for all instructions.

```
always begin : main_process
  if (!reset) begin
     #CYCLE fetch ;
     #CYCLE execute ;
     #CYCLE write_result ;
  end
  else #CYCLE ;
end
```

Figure 3.5 The main process

35

This model assumes that these tasks are sequential and that no pipeline or parallelism is employed. As a result, execution of each instruction takes three cycles to complete. In the next refinement step we shall see the implications of a pipeline architecture.

The reset signal (more accurately, the reset register) is checked to see if the processor is being reset. If so, the main process waits for one iteration cycle before checking the reset signal again. The else clause of the if-then-else statement is needed. Without it, the always process becomes a zero delay infinite loop when reset is high.

System Initialization

The initial state of the simulation model is equivalent to the state of the real hardware at power-on. To initialize the system, the test program is loaded, a monitor is set up, and the reset sequence is applied in the initial block as shown in Figure 3.6. The initial block is executed only once at the start of the simulation.

```
task apply_reset ;
begin
  reset = 1 ;
  #CYCLE
  reset = 0 ;
  pc = 0 ;
end
endtask

initial begin : prog_load
        $readmemb("sisc.prog",MEM) ;
        $monitor("%d %d %h %h %h",$time,pc,
             RFILE[0],RFILE[1],RFILE[2]) ;
        apply_reset ;
end
```

Figure 3.6 Initialization process

The Verilog system task $readmemb is used to load a test program from an ASCII data file into the memory array MEM.

The reset sequence is applied by invoking the apply_reset task (Figure 3.6). The reset sequence is very simple in this example; it toggles the reset signal and sets the program counter to zero.

The $monitor task provides the debugging information about the simulation time, program counter, and selected registers from the register file.

Functions and Tasks

With the declarations, main process, and system initialization in place, the next step is to write the tasks and functions that implement the functionality of the processor. The functions in our description are getsrc, getdst, and checkcond. The tasks are fetch, execute, write_results, set_condcode, clear_condcode, and apply_reset.

The most interesting task is the execute task (see Figure 3.7). It uses a case statement to decode the OPCODE, and provides appropriate action that corresponds to the execution of each individual instruction.

Note the use of symbolic names to access various fields of the instruction register. If the ordering or the length of various fields were to change, these tasks are not affected; only the definitions will need to be changed.

The nop instruction advances the simulation time by one cycle without any other activity. The halt instruction is implemented using the $stop system task. The default action provides the mechanism to catch illegal instructions. The branch instruction illustrates how a function is called in Verilog.

The load and store instructions implement memory access with a simple protocol. Similarly, the shift and rotate instructions implement a fairly complex hardware operation using simple behavioral constructs in Verilog.

The add and multiply instructions at first glance appear very simple. However, that is not the case. The result of adding two numbers can be at most one bit larger than the largest of the two numbers, but the size of the multiplication can be as big as the sum of the sizes of the multiplier and the multiplicand. Assigning the multiplication of two WIDTH size operands to a WIDTH+1 size register (result) saves the least significant WIDTH+1 bits of the result, and only the least significant WIDTH bits are saved in any of the memory or register file locations.

```
task execute ;
begin
  case ('OPCODE)
    'NOP : ;
    'BRA : begin
            if (checkcond('CCODE)) pc = 'DST ;
          end
    'HLT : begin
            $display("Halt ...") ; $stop ;
          end
    'LD :  begin                      load register
            clearcondcode ;
            if ('SRC) RFILE['DST] = 'SRC ;    immediate
            else RFILE['DST] = MEM['SRC] ;
            setcondcode({1'b0,RFILE['DST]}) ;
          end
    'STR : begin
            clearcondcode ;
            if ('SRC) MEM['DST] = 'SRC ;
            else MEM['DST] = RFILE['SRC] ;
          end
    'ADD : begin
            clearcondcode ;
            src1 = getsrc(ir) ;
            src2 = getdst(ir) ;
            result = src1 + src2 ;
            setcondcode(result) ;
          end
            . . .
            . . .
    default: $display("Invalid Opcode found");
  endcase
end
endtask
```

Figure 3.7 The execute task

One solution is to use wider registers (2*WIDTH) for computation, and a register pair or two memory locations for storing the result. Another solution is to restrict the size of the operands to no more than half of the width. Yet another approach is to say that the accuracy of the result is the least significant WIDTH+1 bits. In the SISC example we selected 32-bit accuracy of the result.

It is important to remember that Verilog defines the arithmetic operators so that they carry out all operations in 2's complement representation.

38

A Test Program

Once the model is written, we must prepare a test program to simulate it. A program to count the number of 1's in a binary pattern is used for this purpose. The program, written in binary, is shown in Figure 3.21. The program is stored in the file sisc.prog and is loaded into the memory array mem using the $readmemb system task. A hexadecimal program can be loaded using $readmemh system task.

Running the Model

By executing the test program in our model, we can demonstrate how the instructions are fetched, decoded, and executed, and how the results are stored. This simulation model can now be used to develop other diagnostics, system software, or applications programs for the target hardware. The following command to an operating system prompt will get us started:

```
%verilog sisc_instruction_set_model.v
```

where sisc_instruction_set_model.v is the name of the file that contains the Verilog description of the SISC instruction set model.

There are two distinct phases in simulating a model in the Verilog simulation environment. The first phase is to eliminate all the compilation and linkage errors. The compilation errors are primarily due to syntax errors and undefined structures. The linkage errors are related to port sizes, module instantiation, missing connections, etc.

The syntactically correct Verilog description of a model can now be simulated to verify its functionality. This phase is usually much more time consuming than the first phase. Use of interactive debugging and some proven techniques can help reduce the time spent here. Some useful debugging techniques are discussed later.

Debugging

Although the present model is a good one, only trivial designs require no debugging. In addition to the interactive debugging environment provided by the simulator, we need some tasks customized for testing a model. For our model, it is important to monitor the changes

```
//to display register and memory conduits
task disprm ;
input rm ;
input [ADDRSIZE-1:0] adr1, adr2 ;
begin
  if (rm == 'REGTYPE) begin
    while (adr2 >= adr1) begin
         $display("REGFILE[%d]=%d\n",
                    adr1,RFILE[adr1]) ;
       adr1 = adr1 + 1 ;
    end
  end
  else begin
    while (adr2 >= adr1) begin
       $display("MEM[%d]=%d\n",
                    adr1,MEM[adr1]) ;
       adr1 = adr1 + 1 ;
    end
  end
end
endtask
```

Figure 3.8 A debugging task to dump states

occurring in the value of the program counter and certain registers in the register file.

An example of a task, disprm, to help debugging the model, is shown in Figure 3.8. It is used for displaying the contents of a range of registers or memory locations. It is rather inefficient to type in the body of the task every time there is a need to look at memory locations, say, 20, 21, and 22; issuing separate $display commands is also time consuming when the start and end addresses are more than a few locations apart.

The apply_reset task is useful to "restart" the simulation without having to exit and reenter. It can be made more sophisticated by setting all registers and memory locations to unknowns (x), zero, or a predefined bit pattern. The apply-reset task can also be modified to include the $readmemb system task to load a new program every time a reset is applied to the system.

Modeling Pipeline Control

So far we have modeled the SISC architecture at the instruction set level. Let us now discuss processor control. We introduce the concept of pipeline for a quick reference and to develop a functional model by refining the SISC model just developed.

What Is a Pipeline?

Essentially, pipeline architecture is a way of exploiting inherent parallelism or providing additional resources to create necessary parallelism. A simple pipeline can be built from the inherent concurrency between the fetching of one instruction from memory and the execution of the previously fetched instruction.

In other words, when one instruction is being executed, the next instruction is being fetched. If the next instruction is already available for execution at the end of the current instruction, the processor overlaps the fetch cycle with the execution cycle. This is a typical instruction pipeline.

Figure 3.9 explains how a three-stage pipeline architecture will process the instructions. The stages are fetch(F), execute(E), and write(W). It is assumed that each stage takes one cycle to complete.

```
cycle # Without Pipeline      With Pipeline

   1              F1           F1
   2              E1           F2    E1
   3              W1           F3    E2    W1
   4              F2           F4    E3    W2
   5              E2           F5    E4    W3
   6              W2                 E5    W4
   7              F3                       W5
   8              E3
   9              W3
  10              F4
  11              E4
  12              W4           F12
  13              F5           F13   E12   W11
  14              E5           F14   E13   W12
  15              W5           F15   E14   W13

Without pipeline 5 instructions execute in 15 cycles.
(#instructions)*3

With pipeline 5 instructions execute in 7 cycles.
(#instructions)+2

Legend: F = Fetch,   E = Execute, W = Write
```

Figure 3.9 Tabular representation of a three-stage pipeline

Therefore, a processor without any pipeline requires three cycles to execute one instruction, whereas a processor with a three-stage pipeline can complete, on average, one instruction every cycle. This concept can be extended to more pipeline stages to improve performance.

To improve the performance, we keep the next instruction available for execution (locality of reference). However, there are complications and special cases even in this simple concept. For example, a taken branch causes the next instruction to be an instruction different from the instruction at the next address. Therefore, an instruction that was already fetched (the prefetched instruction) must be discarded, and the instruction from the branched address should be fetched. Since the processor must discard prefetched instruction, the execution unit is idle for one cycle—or as many cycles as it takes to fetch an instruction from memory.

In a processor with a larger number of pipeline stages, more complex steps may be required to ensure the proper completion of all the instructions in the pipeline. This phenomenon is generally referred to as "flushing the pipeline." The halt instruction also flushes the pipeline.

Another circumstance that reduces pipeline efficiency arises during the execution of the load and store instructions. Since these instructions are necessary for accessing memory to transfer data to or from the register file inside the processor, the processor cannot fetch the next instruction. The wasted fetch cycle, in turn, causes a wasted execute cycle if the processor has provision for only one prefetch instruction. The multiported memories and register files are used to keep the pipeline filled.

Functional Partitioning

Now let us improve our earlier SISC design by implementing a three stage pipeline. The three stages of the pipeline are fetch, execute, and write_result. With respect to the instruction currently being executed, the next instruction is being prefetched, and the previous instruction's result is being written in the register file. This is a general scenario that does not hold true for branch, load, and store instructions.

We have simplified the SISC processor pipeline by making it synchronous. As shown in the description in Figure 3.10, three

42

```
always @(posedge clock) begin : phase1_loop
   if (!reset) begin
      fetched = 0 ;
      executed = 0 ;
      if (!queue_full && !mem_access)
         -> do_fetch ;
      if (qsize || mem_access)
         -> do_execute ;
      if (result_ready)
         -> do_write_results ;
   end
end
```

Figure 3.10 Triggering simultaneous events

simultaneous events—do_fetch, do_execute, and do_write_results—are
triggered on the positive edge of the clock (phase 1, if it is a two-phase
clock). The main_process block of the earlier SISC model is modified to
create the phase1_loop block. The negative edge of the clock transfers
information between the pipelines. Additional declarations required to
model the pipeline are shown in Figure 3.11. These registers, wires, and
events are referenced in the subsequent explanation of the pipeline
model.

Note that the order of the if statements in the phase1_loop is not
important because they just trigger the events; the corresponding events

```
parameter  QDEPTH = 3 ;// Instr Queue Depth
//  Instr queue, and instr register for write
reg [WIDTH-1:0]    IR_Queue[0:QDEPTH-1], wir ;

// Copy of result, and Execute and fetch pointers
reg [WIDTH:0]    wresult ;
reg [2:0]        eptr, fptr, qsize ;

// Various Controls/flags
reg      mem_access, branch_taken, halt_found ;
reg      result_ready ;
reg      executed, fetched ;
wire     queue_full ;

event    do_fetch, do_execute, do_write_results ;
```

Figure 3.11 Additional declarations for pipeline modeling

and tasks are not necessarily executed in that order. Each of these events model the activity of the three functional units.

The Fetch Unit

The primary function of the fetch unit is to transfer an instruction from the memory into the processor and make it available to the execution unit. In order to keep the execution unit continuously busy, we need an instruction queue so that instructions may be fetched a priori. This is achieved by using the IR_Queue. We have chosen a queue depth of three to match the number of pipeline stages. A 2-bit register fptr refers to the current position in the IR_Queue where the next fetched instruction is to be stored. The qsize register indicates how many instructions have been prefetched. It is also used to indicate whether IR_Queue is empty or full. If the queue is empty, the execution can not proceed, causing wasted execution cycles and a delay in the pipeline; whereas, if IR_Queue is full, fetching the next instruction will overwrite an instruction which has not yet been executed.

The mem_access flag signals the fetch unit to waste a cycle because a load or a store instruction is in progress. The if statement controlling the do_fetch event reflects this. The fetch task, shown in Figure 3.12, has been modified to save the fetched instruction in the IR_queue instead of loading it directly in the instruction register IR. It also turns on the fetched flag, indicating that a fetch cycle has been completed.

```
task fetch ;
begin
   IR_Queue[fptr] = MEM[pc] ;
   fetched = 1 ;
end
endtask
```

Figure 3.12 The fetch task

The Execution Unit

The execution unit, similar to the one described earlier, decodes the current instruction and executes it. It is assumed that all the instructions, with the exception of load and store instructions, can be executed in one cycle. For the same reason, all SISC instructions are

44

single word instructions and all the arithmetic instructions—add, multiply, complement, shift, and rotate—expect the operands to be immediate (part of the instruction word), or contained in the register file.

Further examination of the arithmetic instructions indicate that the ALU requires two input registers, src1 and src2, and one output register, result. Since the source as well as the destination of every arithmetic instruction deal with the register file, the register file must have three independent ports: two for reading the operands and one for writing the result. Remember that the result of the previous instruction is written in the register file while reading the operands for the current instruction.

The memory is still a scarce resource in our architecture. This effect is modeled in the execution unit as two cycle load and store instructions. The model segment in Figure 3.13 shows how the load instruction is modeled. Upon encountering the load instruction, the execution unit sets mem_access flag to reserve the access to the memory in the next cycle. The fetch unit, in the current cycle, completes reading the next instruction from the memory. The fetch unit is idle in the next cycle, and the execution unit will access the memory. The execution unit, essentially executes the load instruction of the previous cycle, because the instruction register is not loaded with the new instruction when mem_access flag is set. At the end of the memory transaction, the execute unit resets the mem_access flag, allowing the execute unit to get the next instruction from the instruction queue into the instruction register and the fetch unit to fill the instruction queue with new instructions from the memory.

The execution unit wastes a cycle if a branch was taken or the instruction queue was empty. A taken branch and the execution of a halt

```
if (!mem_access) ir = IR_Queue[eptr] ;

'LD : begin
        if (mem_access == 0) // Reserve next
            mem_access = 1 ; // cycle
        else begin    // Mem access
            ....... // in next cycle
        end
    end
```

Figure 3.13 Memory access for load instruction

```
task flush_queue ;
begin
  // pc is already modified by branch execution
  fptr = 0 ;
  eptr = 0 ;
  qsize = 0 ;
  branch_taken = 0 ;
end
endtask
```

Figure 3.14 Flushing the pipeline

instruction are the only two situations that result in an empty instruction queue in the SISC processor. The flush_queue task shown in Figure 3.14 describes the necessary action.

The rest of the model of the execution unit remains unchanged for all the arithmetic instructions as described in the execute task in Figure 3.7. The set_condcode and clear_condcode tasks and the checkcond function are not affected by the pipeline either.

The Write Unit

The execution and the write stages of the pipeline communicate via two registers—wresult and wir. If the result must be written to the register file, the result_ready flag is set by the execution unit. The result from the result register is copied into the wresult register, and the instruction register (ir) is copied into wir. The write unit writes the result from the wresult register into the destination in the register file as indicated by the wir dest field in the next cycle. Since wir is a copy of the instruction that computed the result, the dest field correctly reflects the destination in the register file for the previous instruction.

Notice that we simplified the write unit by copying the current instruction from the ir register to wir register instead of keeping a pointer to the instruction in the instruction queue. The copy_results task in Figure 3.15 describes how the result from the execution unit is transferred to the write unit, and Figure 3.16 shows how the result is written in the destination register.

Two alternate approaches that use more complex logic can alleviate the need for copying the result from the result register into the

```
task copy_results ;
begin
  if (('OPCODE >= 'ADD) && ('OPCODE < 'HLT))begin
      setcondcode(result) ;
      wresult = result ;
      wir = ir ;
      result_ready = 1 ;
  end
end
endtask
```

Figure 3.15 Copying result and instruction

```
task write_result ;
begin
  if (('WOPCODE>='ADD) && ('WOPCODE<'HLT)) begin
      if ('WDSTTYPE == 'REGTYPE)
            RFILE['WDST] = wresult ;
      else MEM['WDST] = wresult ;
      result_ready = 0 ;
  end
end
endtask
```

Figure 3.16 Writing result in the register file

result register. One possibility is to modify the result register in the negative clock cycle by the execution unit and copy it into the register file in the positive half of the next cycle by the write unit. Another possibility is to remove the write stage of the pipeline completely and write the result from the ALU directly in the register file. Appropriate simulation analysis can be used to arrive at and justify such decisions.

Phase-2 Control Operations

Overall, the SISC processor is a synchronous design. The functional blocks, described above, correspond to the three stages of the pipeline. They operate in the positive half of the clock cycle. In the negative half of the clock cycle:

47

- the program counter (pc) is updated based on whether the branch was taken or not.

- condition codes are set from the newly computed result.

- the instruction register (ir) and the result register are copied to their shadow registers (the wir and the wresult registers respectively).

- the fetch and the execute reference pointers (eptr and fptr) to the instruction queue are updated.

These actions are shown in Figure 3.17 by the set_pointers task and the phase2_loop process.

```
task set_pointers ;      // Manage queue pointers
begin
   case ({fetched,executed})
   2'b00 : ;            // idle fetch cycle
   2'b01 : begin        // No fetch
             qsize = qsize - 1 ;
             eptr = (eptr + 1)%QDEPTH ;
           end
   2'b10 : begin        // No execute
             qsize = qsize + 1 ;
             fptr = (fptr + 1) % QDEPTH ;
           end
   2'b11 : begin        // Fetch and execute
             eptr = (eptr + 1)%QDEPTH ;
             fptr = (fptr + 1) % QDEPTH ;
           end
   endcase
end
endtask

always @(negedge clock) begin : phase2_loop
  if (!reset) begin
    if (!mem_access && !branch_taken)
       copy_results ;
    if (branch_taken) pc = 'DST ;
    else if (!mem_access) pc = pc+1; ...
    if (branch_taken || halt_found)
       flush_queue ;
    else set_pointers ;
    if (halt_found) begin
       $stop ;
       halt_found = 0 ;
    end
  end
end
```

Figure 3.17 Phase-2 control operations

The instruction queue requires flushing, which is postponed until the negative half of the cycle because the instructions in the pipeline must be allowed to complete. For the same reason, the simulation of the effect of the halt instruction is not stopped until all the activities in the negative half of the cycle are done. This allows the write unit to store the result of the previous instruction in the positive half of the next cycle when the execution unit sets up the 1-bit halt_found flag.

The Interlock Problem

There is a problem in the pipeline architecture model that is not apparent. The problem, usually referred to as "register interlock," appears when an instruction that modifies the contents of a register in the register file is followed by another instruction that attempts to read the same register. The manifestation of this behavior can be more complex and difficult to recognize in an architecture with more pipelined stages.

The register interlock situation is best explained by an example. Consider the two program segments shown in Figure 3.18. In program segment 1, there is no contention of the resource, the R2 register in the register file, provided the register file is multiported.

```
         Program Segment 1


I1:     ADD     R1, R2  // R1 = R1 + R2
I2:     CMP     R3, R2  // R3 = ~R2


         Program Segment 2


I3:     ADD     R1, R2  // R1 = R1 + R2
I4:     CMP     R3, R1  // R3 = ~R1
```

Figure 3.18 The interlock problem

The scenario changes in program segment 2. The first instruction (I3) reads two registers (R1 and R2) from the register file and writes the result of the addition in register R1. The second instruction (I4) reads the value of register R1 and stores its complement in R3. Due to the concurrency between the execution unit and the write unit, the execution unit may read an incorrect value of R1 while executing I4. (The result of I3 would be in the process of being written to the register R1.)

If the value of R1 is read before the write is complete, I4 will operate on the previous value of register R1. In the real hardware, this could be a hazard or a race condition, depending on the implementation of the read and the write operation for the multiported register file. Two alternate solutions to the problem are discussed below.

The simplest solution is to insert the nop instruction between the pair of instructions that cause register interlock. The advantage is that no modification of the architecture and the design is required. The disadvantage, however, is the execution of additional instructions, wasting one cycle for every register interlock and reducing the throughput. It would also require modification of the software, in particular the SISC compiler and the optimizer. The modified program segment 2 is shown in Figure 3.19.

```
I3:     ADD     R1, R2  // R1 = R1 + R2
IX:     NOP             // Avoid interlock
I4:     CMP     R3, R1  // R3 = ~R1
```

Figure 3.19 Modified program segment 2

An alternate approach is to implement additional logic in the design such that the register interlock conditions are recognized. Upon recognizing the situation, the hardware can copy the contents of the result register from the previous instruction to one of the operands (src1 or src2) for the current instruction. Simultaneously, reading the operand from the interlocking register must be prevented to avoid overwriting with an incorrect value. This is known as the "bypassing" technique. The model segment shown in Figure 3.20 implements the bypassing in SISC to remove the interlocking problem.

Similar care should be taken for the interlock created when the destination register of an instruction is used as the source for the store instruction that follows immediately. Simulation analysis should be used in conjunction with the design goals to decide which alternative to implement.

```
reg      bypass ;

function [31:0] getsrc;
input [31:0] i ;
begin
    if (bypass)  getsrc = result ;
    else if (`SRCTYPE === `REGTYPE)
            getsrc = RFILE[`SRC] ;
    else getsrc = `SRC ;    // immediate type
end
endfunction

function [31:0] getdst;
input [31:0] i ;
begin
    if (bypass)  getdst = result ;
    else if (`DSTTYPE === `REGTYPE)
            getdst = RFILE[`DST] ;
    else $display("Error : Immediate data
            cannot be destination.") ;
end
endfunction

always @(do_execute) begin : execute_block
    if (!mem_access) begin
        ir = IR_Queue[eptr] ;
        bypass = ((`SRC == `WDST) ||
                  (`DST == `WDST)) ;
    end
    execute ;
    if (!mem_access) executed = 1 ;
end
```

Figure 3.20 Modified functions and execute process for bypass

Test Vector Generation

Once a model of any system is developed, it is important to test it in order to establish its validity. Some nontrivial problems related to the architecture or the implementation, such as the register interlock, are uncovered during testing. This is equally true with models of a simple NAND gate, to a complex microprocessor, and to much more complicated microprocessor-based computer systems and even networks of such systems. Simple techniques are applied when the models are small, easy to comprehend, and exhaustive testing is possible. In the case of complex systems, it is not always possible to generate all possible

51

combinations. Rather, a large number of diagnostic programs are used as test vectors to test certain sections of the system.

These diagnostic programs can be written in a high level programming language such as C, and a compiler written for the target system can generate corresponding object code (machine code). If a compiler is not available, a simple assembler for the target instruction set can be used to generate machine code from hand-coded assembly language programs. Such tools ease the cumbersome, time-consuming, and error-prone task of creating test vectors in 1's and 0's. A further disadvantage of hand-coding is often learned through painful experience when the instruction format (order of various instruction fields) changes.

Once the diagnostic program has been translated to a sequence of instructions, it is loaded into the simulation model's memory, just as an executable program is loaded into the system's memory. Applying a reset to the system starts the instruction fetch with the first instruction pointed to by the program counter. The instruction itself is equivalent to applying an external test vector to the pins of the processor. The execution of the instruction inside the processor controls the fetching of the subsequent instructions (test vectors).

The Verilog-XL simulator can load a diagnostic program saved in an ASCII file, into a simulated memory by using one of the two system tasks: $readmemb or $readmemh. The $readmemb task is used when the instructions are represented in binary, and $readmemh is used when the instructions are represented in hex. The program file may contain comments, underbars (_), and white space to enhance readability.

Typically, the program is loaded in the simulated memory at the beginning of a simulation run. This is done using the $readmemb system task in an initial statement. (See the block labeled prog_load in Figure 3.6). A sample program that computes the number of 1's in a binary number is shown in Figure 3.21. Here, the end of the program is indicated by stopping the simulation for possible examination of registers, memory locations, and other signals and variables. In order to speed up the process of verifying an error-free execution of the program, it is a common practice to check computed results against the expected results. In a diagnostic program consisting of hundreds or thousands of instructions, such comparisons may be scattered throughout many parts of the program.

```
// Program to count  number of 1's in a given binary number.
//
0010_1000_0000_0000_0000_0000_0000_0001 //LD R1,#0
0010_0000_0000_0000_1001_0000_0000_0000 //LD R2,NMBR
0001_0010_0000_0000_0000_0000_0000_0100 //STRT:BRA L1
0100_1000_0000_0000_0001_0000_0000_0001 //ADD R1,#1
0111_1000_0000_0000_0001_0000_0000_0000 //L1:SHF R2, #1
0001_0100_0000_0000_0000_0000_0000_0111 //BRA L2, ZERO
0001_0000_0000_0000_0000_0000_0000_0010 //BRA STRT, ALW
0011_0000_0000_0000_0001_0000_0000_1010 //L2:STR RSLT,R2
1001_1111_1111_1111_1111_1111_1111_1111 //HLT
0101_0101_0101_0101_1010_1010_1010_1010 //NMBR:5555aaaa
0000_0000_0000_0000_0000_0000_0000_0000 //RSLT:00000000
```

Figure 3.21 An assembly language program as test vectors

When the simulation model is very large, leaving and reentering the simulator to load a new diagnostic program can be very time-consuming. If the behavior of a reset is modeled to bring the machine to its initial state, the $readmemb system task can be used interactively to load a new program at the end of the current program.

Summary

This chapter presented how to model a VLSI processor in Verilog HDL. The model was refined from its initial architectural description without a pipeline to a high level functional description with three stages of pipeline. The register interlock problem was discussed at length to show the usefulness of simulation in solving problems or making design decisions. Concepts of test vector creation were also presented.

The complete Verilog HDL descriptions of both the models are provided in the following Figure 3.22. Its first part shows declarations, functions, and tasks common to both the models. The next part shows the nonpipelined model followed by the pipelined model.

```
/*
 * Declarations, functions, and tasks
 * These are common to all models of SISC.
 *
 * sisc_declarations.v
 *
 * %W% %G%   --  for  version control
 */

// Declare parameters

parameter CYCLE = 10 ;              // Cycle Time
parameter WIDTH = 32 ;             // Width of datapaths
parameter ADDRSIZE = 12 ;         // Size of address fields
parameter MEMSIZE = (1<<ADDRSIZE);// Size of max memory
parameter MAXREGS = 16 ;          // Maximum registers
parameter SBITS = 5 ;             // Status register bits

// Declare Registers and Memory

reg [WIDTH-1:0] MEM[0:MEMSIZE-1], // Memory
                RFILE[0:MAXREGS-1], // Register File
                ir, // Instruction Regsiter
                src1, src2 ; // Alu operation registers
reg [WIDTH:0]   result ; // ALU result register
reg [SBITS-1:0] psr ; // Processor Status Register
reg [ADDRSIZE-1:0] pc ; // Program counter
reg             dir ; // rotate direction
reg             reset ; // System Reset
integer         i ; // useful for interactive debugging

// General definitions

`define TRUE    1
`define FALSE   0

`define DEBUG_ON      debug = 1
`define DEBUG_OFF     debug = 0

// Define Instruction fields

`define OPCODE   ir[31:28]
`define SRC      ir[23:12]
`define DST      ir[11:0]
`define SRCTYPE  ir[27] //source type,0=reg (mem for LD),1=imm
`define DSTTYPE  ir[26] //destination type, 0=reg, 1=imm
`define CCODE    ir[27:24]
`define SRCNT    ir[23:12]//Shift/rotate count -=left, +=right

// Operand Types

`define REGTYPE    0
`define IMMTYPE    1
```

```
// Define opcodes for each instruction

`define NOP       4'b0000
`define BRA       4'b0001
`define LD        4'b0010
`define STR       4'b0011
`define ADD       4'b0100
`define MUL       4'b0101
`define CMP       4'b0110
`define SHF       4'b0111
`define ROT       4'b1000
`define HLT       4'b1001

// Define Condition Code fields

`define CARRY     psr[0]
`define EVEN      psr[1]
`define PARITY    psr[2]
`define ZERO      psr[3]
`define NEG       psr[4]

// Define Condition Codes

                        // Condition Code set when ...
`define CCC       0     // Result has carry
`define CCE       1     // Result is even
`define CCP       2     // Result has odd parity
`define CCZ       3     // Result is Zero
`define CCN       4     // Result is Negative
`define CCA       5     // Always

`define RIGHT     0     // Rotate/Shift Right
`define LEFT      1     // Rotate/Shift Left

// Functions for ALU operands and result

function [WIDTH-1:0] getsrc;
input [WIDTH-1:0] in ;
begin
  if (`SRCTYPE === `REGTYPE) begin
     getsrc = RFILE[`SRC] ;
  end
  else begin // immediate type
     getsrc = `SRC ;
  end
end
endfunction

function [WIDTH-1:0] getdst;
input [WIDTH-1:0] in ;
begin
  if (`DSTTYPE === `REGTYPE) begin
     getdst = RFILE[`DST] ;
  end
  else begin // immediate type
     $display("Error:Immediate data cant be destination.");
```

55

```
      end
   end
endfunction

// Functions/tasks for Condition Codes

function checkcond;      // Returns 1 if condition code is set.
input [4:0] ccode ;
begin
   case (ccode)
     `CCC : checkcond = `CARRY ;
     `CCE : checkcond = `EVEN ;
     `CCP : checkcond = `PARITY ;
     `CCZ : checkcond = `ZERO ;
     `CCN : checkcond = `NEG ;
     `CCA : checkcond = 1 ;
   endcase
end
endfunction

task clearcondcode ;     // Reset condition codes in PSR.
begin
   psr = 0 ;
end
endtask

task setcondcode ;       // Compute the condition codes and set
PSR.
input [WIDTH:0] res ;
begin
   `CARRY = res[WIDTH] ;       33rd bit
   `EVEN  = ~res[0] ;          1st bit
   `PARITY = ^res ;
   `ZERO  = ~(|res) ;
   `NEG = res[WIDTH-1] ;       32nd bit
end
endtask

/* ==================================================
 *
 *   Model of SISC without piepline.
 *
 *   sisc_instruction_set_model.v
 *
 *   Useful for instruction set simulation.
 *   Three main tasks - fetch, execute, write.
 *
 *   %W% %G%  --  For version control
 */

module instruction_set_model ;

// Include sisc_declarations.v file here.
// All common declarations, functions, and tasks go here.
// The rest of the model appears below.
```

```
// Main Tasks - fetch, execute, write_result

task fetch ;      // Fetch the instruction and increment PC.
begin
  ir = MEM[pc] ;
  pc = pc + 1 ;
end
endtask

task execute ;   // Decode and execute the instruction.
begin
  case (`OPCODE)
    `NOP : ;
    `BRA :begin
              if (checkcond(`CCODE) == 1) pc = `DST ;
          end
    `LD : begin
              clearcondcode ;
              if (`SRC) RFILE[`DST] = `SRC ;
              else RFILE[`DST] = MEM[`SRC] ;
              setcondcode({1'b0,RFILE[`DST]}) ;
          end
    `STR :begin
              clearcondcode ;
              if (`SRC) MEM[`DST] = `SRC ;
              else MEM[`DST] = RFILE[`SRC] ;
          end
    `ADD :begin
              clearcondcode ;
              src1 = getsrc(ir) ;
              src2 = getdst(ir) ;
              result = src1 + src2 ;
              setcondcode(result) ;
          end
    `MUL :begin
              clearcondcode ;
              src1 = getsrc(ir) ;
              src2 = getdst(ir) ;
              result = src1 * src2 ;
              setcondcode(result) ;
          end
    `CMP :begin
              clearcondcode ;
              src1 = getsrc(ir) ;
              result = ~src1 ;
              setcondcode(result) ;
          end
    `SHF :begin
              clearcondcode ;
              src1 = getsrc(ir) ;
              src2 = getdst(ir) ;
              i = src1[ADDRSIZE-1:0] ;
              result = (i>=0) ? (src2 >> i) : (src2 << -i);
              setcondcode(result) ;
```

shift right   *shift left*

57

```
            end
    `ROT :begin                 count
                clearcondcode ;
                src1 = getsrc(ir) ;
                src2 = getdst(ir) ;
                dir = (src1[ADDRSIZE-1]==0) ? `RIGHT : `LEFT ;
                i = (src1[ADDRSIZE-1]==0) ?
                    src1 : -src1[ADDRSIZE-1:0];    make positive
                while (i > 0) begin
                    if (dir == `RIGHT) begin
                        result = src2 >> 1 ;
                        result[WIDTH-1] = src2[0] ;
                    end
                    else begin
                        result = src2 << 1 ;
                        result[0] = src2[WIDTH-1] ;
                    end
                    i = i - 1 ;
                    src2 = result ;
                end
                setcondcode(result) ;
            end
    `HLT :begin
                $display("Halt ...") ;
                $stop ;
            end
    default : $display("Error : Illegal Opcode.") ;
  endcase
end
endtask

// Write the result in register file or memory.
task write_result ;
begin
  if ((`OPCODE >= `ADD) && (`OPCODE < `HLT)) begin
      if (`DSTTYPE == `REGTYPE) RFILE[`DST] = result ;
      else MEM[`DST] = result ;
  end
end
endtask


//  Debugging help ....

task apply_reset ;
begin
  reset = 1 ;
  #CYCLE
  reset = 0 ;
  pc = 0 ;
end
endtask

task disprm ;
input rm ;
input [ADDRSIZE-1:0] adr1, adr2 ;
```

```
begin
  if (rm == `REGTYPE) begin
     while (adr2 >= adr1) begin
        $display("REGFILE[%d]=%d\n",adr1,RFILE[adr1]) ;
        adr1 = adr1 + 1 ;
     end
  end
  else begin
     while (adr2 >= adr1) begin
        $display("MEM[%d]=%d\n",adr1,MEM[adr1]) ;
        adr1 = adr1 + 1 ;
     end
  end
end
endtask

// Initial and always blocks

initial begin : prog_load
   $readmemb("sisc.prog",MEM) ;
   $monitor("%d %d %h %h %h",
         $time,pc,RFILE[0],RFILE[1],RFILE[2]);
   apply_reset ;
end

always begin : main_process
  if (!reset) begin
     #CYCLE fetch ;
     #CYCLE execute ;
     #CYCLE write_result ;
  end
  else #CYCLE ;
end
endmodule

/* =====================================
 *
 * Model of SISC processor with pipeline
 *
 * sisc_pipeline_model.v
 *
 * %W%  %G%  -- For version control
 */

module pipeline_control ;

// All declarations, functions, and tasks made before
// should be included here. In addition, the following
// declarations and definitions are used just for the
// pipeline control modeling.

// Declare parameters

parameter HALFCYCLE = (CYCLE/2) ; // Half Cycle Time
parameter QDEPTH = 3 ;            // Instruction Queue Depth
```

[handwritten annotations: execute ptr (execute this instruction), fetch ptr (place for fetch instruction)]

```
// Declare additional registers for pipeline control

reg [WIDTH-1:0] IR_Queue[0:QDEPTH-1],    // Instruction Queue
                wir; // Instruction Regsiter for write stage
reg [2:0]       eptr, fptr, qsize ; // Book keeping pointers
reg             clock ; // System Clock
reg [WIDTH:0] wresult ; // Alu result register for write stage

// Various Flags - control lines

reg             mem_access, branch_taken, halt_found ;
reg             result_ready ;
reg             executed, fetched ;
reg             debug ;

wire            queue_full ;

event           do_fetch, do_execute, do_write_results ;

// Define Instruction fields

`define WOPCODE  wir[31:28]
`define WDST     wir[11:0]
`define WDSTTYPE wir[26] // destination type, 0=reg, 1=imm

// Continuous assignment for queue_full

assign  queue_full = (qsize == QDEPTH) ;
```
[handwritten annotation: whenever changes]
```
// Functions and Tasks

task fetch ;
begin
  IR_Queue[fptr] = MEM[pc] ;
  fetched = 1 ;
end
endtask

task execute ;
begin
  if (!mem_access) ir = IR_Queue[eptr] ; // New IR required?

  case (`OPCODE)
    `NOP : begin
            if (debug) $display("Nop ...") ;
          end
    `BRA : begin
            if (debug) $write("Branch ...") ;
            if (checkcond(`CCODE) == 1) begin
              pc = `DST ;
              branch_taken = 1 ;
            end
          end
    `LD : begin
          if (mem_access == 0) begin
            mem_access = 1 ; // Reserve next cycle
```

```
                        end
                    else begin // Mem access
                        if (debug) $display("Load ...") ;
                        clearcondcode ;
                        if ('SRCTYPE) begin
                            RFILE['DST] = 'SRC ;
                        end
                        else RFILE['DST] = MEM['SRC] ;
                            setcondcode({1'b0,RFILE['DST]}) ;
                            mem_access = 0 ;
                        end
                    end
            'STR : begin
                        if (mem_access == 0) begin
                            mem_access = 1 ; // Reserve next cycle
                        end
                        else begin // Mem access
                            if (debug) $display("Store ...") ;
                            clearcondcode ;
                            if ('SRCTYPE) begin
                                MEM['DST] = 'SRC ;
                            end
                            else MEM['DST] = RFILE['SRC] ;
                                mem_access = 0 ;
                        end
                    end


                    // ADD, MUL, CMP, SHF, and ROT
                    // are modeled identical to the other model.

            'HLT : begin
                        $display("Halt ...") ;
                        halt_found = 1 ;
                    end
            default : $display("Error:Wrong Opcode in instruction.");
            endcase
            if (!mem_access) executed = 1 ; // Instruction executed?
end
endtask

task write_result ;
begin
    if (('WOPCODE >= 'ADD) && ('WOPCODE < 'HLT)) begin
        if ('WDSTTYPE == 'REGTYPE) RFILE['WDST] = wresult ;
        else MEM['WDST] = wresult ;
        result_ready = 0 ;
    end
end
endtask

task flush_queue ;
begin
    // pc is already modified by branch execution
    fptr = 0 ;
    eptr = 0 ;
    qsize = 0 ;
```

```
      branch_taken = 0 ;
   end
   endtask

   task copy_results ;
   begin
      if (('OPCODE >= 'ADD) && ('OPCODE < 'HLT)) begin
         setcondcode(result) ;
         wresult = result ;
         wir = ir ;
         result_ready = 1 ;
      end
   end
   endtask

   task set_pointers ;              // Manage queue pointers
   begin
      case (({fetched,executed}))
      2'b00 : ;
      2'b01 : begin                  // No fetch
                 qsize = qsize - 1 ;
                 eptr = (eptr + 1)%QDEPTH ;
              end
      2'b10 : begin                  // No execute
                 qsize = qsize + 1 ;
                 fptr = (fptr + 1) % QDEPTH ;
              end
      2'b11 : begin                  // Fetch and execute
                 eptr = (eptr + 1)%QDEPTH ;
                 fptr = (fptr + 1) % QDEPTH ;
              end
      endcase
   end
   endtask

   // Debugging help ....

   task disprm ;
   input rm ;
   input [ADDRSIZE-1:0] adr1, adr2 ;
   begin
     if (rm == 'REGTYPE) begin
        while (adr2 >= adr1) begin
           $display("REGFILE[%d]=%d\n",adr1,RFILE[adr1]) ;
           adr1 = adr1 + 1 ;
        end
     end
     else begin
        while (adr2 >= adr1) begin
           $display("MEM[%d]=%d\n",adr1,MEM[adr1]) ;
           adr1 = adr1 + 1 ;
        end
     end
   end
   endtask
```

```
task  apply_reset;        // Reset the system
begin
  reset = 1 ;
  @(negedge clock) #1 ;
  reset = 0 ;
  pc = 0 ;
  mem_access = 0 ;
  branch_taken = 0 ;
  halt_found = 0 ;
  qsize = 0 ;
  result_ready = 0 ;
  eptr = 0 ;
  fptr = 0 ;
  executed = 0 ;
  fetched = 0 ;
end
endtask

// Initial and Always Blocks ...

initial begin : setup_and_prog_load
   `DEBUG_OFF ;
   waves ;
   $readmemb("rsisc.prog",MEM) ;
   apply_reset ;
end

initial begin : clock_loop       // clock loop
   clock = 1 ;
   forever begin
      #(HALFCYCLE) clock = ~clock ;
   end
end

always @(posedge clock) begin : phase1_loop
   if (!reset) begin
      fetched = 0 ; executed = 0 ;
      if (!queue_full && !mem_access) -> do_fetch ;
      if (qsize || mem_access)        -> do_execute ;
      if (result_ready)               -> do_write_results ;
   end
end

always @(negedge clock) begin : phase2_loop
   if (!reset) begin
      // Copy results, set condition codes
      if (!mem_access && !branch_taken)
         copy_results ;
      if (branch_taken) pc = `DST ; // Set next PC
      else if (!mem_access)
         pc = pc+1; // No change for idle cycle
      if (branch_taken || halt_found) // Flush Queue
         flush_queue ;
      else set_pointers ; // or adjust pointers
      if (halt_found) begin // Halt?
         $stop ;
```

(handwritten margin notes:) if mem_access then will be done in execute; qsize ≥ 1 ⇒ instructions in queue; like 3 independent processes

63

```
          halt_found = 0 ; // Reset halt
        end
    end
end

// The 3 stages of pipeline are controlled by these events

// Fetch stage

always @(do_fetch) begin : fetch_block
        fetch ;
end

// Execute stage

always @(do_execute) begin : execute_block
  execute ;
end

// Write stage

always @(do_write_results) begin : write_block
    write_result ;
end

endmodule
```

Figure 3.22 SISC pipeline model in Verilog

4

Modeling System Blocks

In the previous chapter we saw how to model a processor at the instruction set level and its function at the behavioral level. In this chapter we present a structural model of the SISC processor and show how to model its various building blocks. We begin with the block diagram of the SISC processor and present its corresponding structural model to show the interconnections of its building blocks. In subsequent sections we develop functional models for these blocks, namely, the datapath, the memory elements, the clock generator, and the control unit.

In the datapath section we present an incrementer, an adder, a barrel shifter, and a multiplier. The section on memories includes a register file, a random-access memory, and a content-addressable memory. The clock generator section includes a single- and a two-phase clock generator. In the last section we present a state machine model of the nonpipelined version of the processor control unit.

Structural Model

We take the pipelined SISC processor model of the previous chapter and proceed to realize the description in hardware. First, we need to identify all the data paths such as registers, counters, the register file, and the arithmetic-logic unit (ALU). Next, we need to identify all the control paths, such as programmable-logic arrays (PLAs) and random logic, that implement various state machines. Having done that, we choose these basic building blocks to construct our data and control paths, and interconnect them to achieve the desired functionality. (A synthesis program is an extremely useful and time-saving tool at this stage; however, discussion of synthesis is outside the scope of this book.)

Most of the datapath elements are easily identified. We need memory with 4K 32-bit words, a register file with two read ports and one write port, a 12-bit register for a program counter (PC), a 32-bit instruction register (IR), a 5-bit processor status register (PSR), and a 32-bit ALU. In addition, implementing the pipeline requires the instruction queue, the registers (fptr and eptr) to indicate the status of various instructions in the pipeline, and the registers to retain the result for latter use (wir and wresult). As you can see, the declarations in the functional model form the basis for identifying the datapath elements.

The control paths are harder to identify. A simple approach is to take all the control signals required by the datapath elements for proper operation and create one control module. Such a control module can be split hierarchically into separate control blocks such as a memory control block, a branch detection block, an instruction queue management block, and so on. Each control block can be of varying complexity, from a handful of simple equations to one or more state machines that require detailed microprogramming.

A block diagram which interconnects the functional blocks of the SISC is presented in Figure 4.1.

A complete Verilog description of the SISC model created from instantiating the lower-level building blocks is shown in Figure 4.2. In order to keep it simple, we have not included the instruction queue in the model.

Datapath

The arithmetic-logic unit of a typical processor performs all the arithmetic, logic, and shift/rotate functions. The arithmetic functions generally include addition, subtraction, multiplication, division, increment, and possibly others. The logic functions consist of AND, OR, NOT, and so forth. The special functions include shift, rotate, and comparison operations. The overall functionality of the ALU, however, is determined by the instruction set as defined by its architecture.

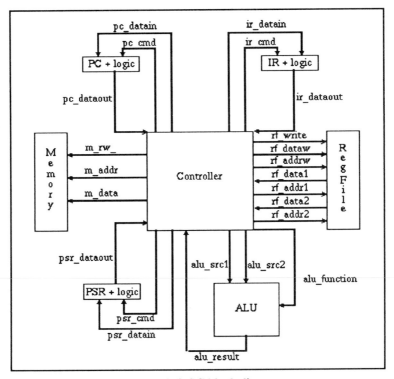

Figure 4.1 SISC block diagram

Referring to Figure 4.3, the datapath of the SISC processor is required to implement the following instructions:

```
ADD,  SUB,  MUL,  CMP    (arithmetic)

SHF,  ROT                (shift, rotate)
```

```
module system ;
parameter ADDRSIZE  = 12,
          WIDTH     = 32 ;
defparam  PSR.WIDTH = 5,
          PC.WIDTH  = 12,
          IR.WIDTH  = 32 ;
wire   phase1, phase2,
       m_rw_, rf_write,
       halt, reset ;
                                    (continued)
```

```
// Commands: Hold, Clear, Load, CountUp
wire [1:0]  ir_cmd, pc_cmd, psr_cmd ;

// NOP, ADD, MUL, CMP, SHF, ROT
wire [3:0]  alu_function ;

// PSR Flags - C, E, P, Z, N
wire [4:0]  psr_dataout, psr_datain ;

wire [ADDRSIZE-1:0]
      pc_addrout,
      pc_addrin,
      m_addr,
      rf_addrw,
      rf_addr1,
      rf_addr2 ;
wire [WIDTH-1:0] m_data,
      ir_dataout,
      ir_datain,
      rf_dataw,
      rf_data1,
      rf_data2,
      alu_src1,
      alu_src2 ;
wire [WIDTH:0] alu_result ;

// Instantiate predefined building blocks

clock   CLK (phase1, phase2) ;
memory  MEM (phase1, phase2, m_data, m_addr, m_rw_) ;
regfile RFILE(phase1, phase2, rf_dataw,
            rf_addrw, rf_write,
            rf_data1, rf_addr1, rf_data2, rf_addr2) ;
regcntr PC  (phase1, phase2, pc_addrout,
            pc_addrin, pc_cmd, reset) ;
regcntr IR  (phase1, phase2, ir_dataout,
            ir_datain, ir_cmd, reset) ;
regcntr PSR (phase1, phase2, psr_dataout,
            psr_datain, psr_cmd, reset) ;
alu     ALU (phase1, phase2, alu_result,
            alu_function, alu_src1, alu_src2) ;
cntrl   CONTROLLER (phase1, phase2,
            halt, reset, m_data, m_addr, m_rw_,
            rf_dataw, rf_addrw, rf_write,
            rf_data1, rf_addr1, rf_data2, rf_addr2,
            pc_addrout, pc_addrin, pc_cmd,
            ir_dataout, ir_datain, ir_cmd,
            psr_dataout, psr_datain, psr_cmd,
            alu_result, alu_function, alu_src1,alu_src2);
endmodule
```

Figure 4.2 Structural model of the processor

A block diagram of the datapath, as it is normally laid out in a VLSI processor design, is shown in Figure 4.3. One side of the datapath receives all the data inputs while the opposite side provides all the data outputs. The control signals are orthogonal to the flow of data in the datapath.

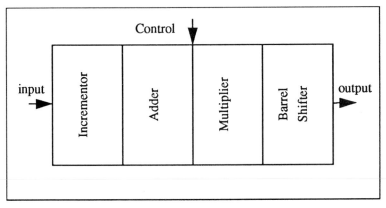

Figure 4.3 Block diagram of the datapath

The input to the datapath consists of two 32-bit data buses. Some instructions require only one data bus while other instructions use both the buses. The datapath blocks necessary to implement the SISC processor instructions are an adder, a multiplier, and a barrel shifter. The incrementer block of the datapath is used to update the value of the program counter.

In the following sections we will model each of these functional blocks of the datapath.

Incrementer

Figure 4.4 gives the model of the incrementer. It implements the incrementer function as a conditional operator which either increments the input or transfers the value unmodified to the output, depending on the value of the control signal. The carry flag is set if the control increments the input and if the output is zero.

A decrement function can be obtained by making minor modifications to the incrementor model as follows:

69

```
wire [31:0] out =
        (control === INCR) ? (in + 1) : in
        (control === DECR) ? (in - 1) : in;
```

This, however, requires that the control signal be 2 bits wide. The set_flags module sets various condition codes in the processor status register.

```
module increment (in, control, out,
                    Nflag, Pflag, Eflag, Zflag, Cflag);
input  [31:0] in;    // input operand
input  control;      // increment or pass
output [31:0] out;   // result operand
output Eflag, Zflag, Cflag, Nflag, Pflag;

parameter LOAD  = 0 ,
          INCR  = 1 ,
          TRUE  = 1 ,
          FALSE = 0 ;

  wire [31:0] out =
          (control === INCR) ? (in + 1) : in;

  wire Cflag =
          (~(|out) && control)  ? TRUE  : FALSE;

  //  set condition codes -- remaining flags
  set_flags  U1(out, Nflag, Pflag, Eflag, Zflag);

endmodule
```

Figure 4.4 Model of the incrementer

Adder

Figure 4.5 represents a high-level abstraction of the adder behavior. The adder implements the ADD and SUB instructions of the datapath. The control signal selects between addition and subtraction in the conditional expression. Various condition codes are set by the set_flags module.

The adder described in Figure 4.5 uses only the "+" operator and does not provide an insight into the internals of its implementation. The carry-look-ahead adder of Figure 4.6 describes a model of what may be an inefficient carry-look-ahead adder. This model uses continuous

```
module adder (operand1,operand2,result,control,
              Cflag, Pflag, Eflag, Zflag, Nflag);

input   [31:0] operand1, operand2;
input   control;
output  [31:0] result;
output  Cflag, Pflag, Eflag, Zflag, Nflag;

parameter ADD  = 0 ,
          SUB  = 1 ;

  assign {Cflag, result} = (control === ADD) ?
                          (operand1 + operand2)  :
                          (operand1 - operand2)  ;

  //  set condition codes -- remaining flags
  set_flags  U2(result, Nflag, Pflag, Eflag, Zflag);

endmodule
```

Figure 4.5 Model of the adder

assignments to generate the 32-bit carry-generate and carry-propagate signals. A for-loop is used to calculate the ripple-carry chain where each bit of the carry chain depends upon its associated carry-generate, carry-propagate, and the carry output from the previous bit.

In an actual implementation of a 32-bit adder, a 32-bit ripple chain would not be used because of the long propagation delay of the carry. Instead, it would use multiple levels of 8-bit ripple-carry adders with carry-look-ahead. Using the technique described here, models can be developed which correspond to the actual implementation.

Barrel Shifter

The shift and rotate (SHF, ROT) instructions of the datapath are modeled by the barrel shifter of Figure 4.7. The barrel shifter models the two rotate and two shift functions: shift-left, shift-right, rotate-left, and rotate-right. The rotation is modeled by repeated shift operations.

Multiplier

The multiplication of two data operands in Verilog can be simply written by using the "*" arithmetic operator. Figure 4.8 models the multiplier which implements the MUL instruction of the datapath. Both

```
module adder_c (operand1,operand2,cin,result,cout);

input   [31:0]  operand1, operand2 ;
input   cin ;
output  [31:0]  result ;
output  cout        ;

reg     [31:0]  carrychain;

// Generate carry
wire    [31:0]  g = operand1 & operand2 ;

// Propagate carry
wire    [31:0]  p = operand1 ^ operand2 ;

always @(operand1 or operand2 or cin)
  begin :carry_generation
    integer i;
    carrychain[0] = g[0] + (p[0] & cin );
    for (i = 1; i <= 31; i = i + 1) begin
      #0 // force evaluation
      carrychain[i] = g[i] + (p[i] & carrychain[i-1]);
    end
  end

wire    [32:0]  shiftedcarry = {carrychain, cin} ;

// Compute the sum
wire    [31:0]  result = p ^ shiftedcarry;

// Carry out
wire    cout = shiftedcarry[32];

endmodule
```

Figure 4.6 Model of the carry-look-ahead adder

the operands of the multiplier are 16-bits wide so as to obtain a 32-bit result. Having 32-bit operands would require the processor either to have a 64-bit data bus or to multiplex the data in two consecutive cycles. This would increase the complexity of the instruction set and require the processor to support multiple cycle operations.

Setting Condition Codes

In modeling the datapath, we saw that each module needs to set the flags for individual condition codes of the processor status register, PSR. Instead of replicating the code in each of the modules, the code is encapsulated in a single module (set_flags) and is instantiated by the individual modules of the datapath.

In the set_flags module of Figure 4.9, the negative flag is the value of the most significant bit of the data value. The parity flag checks for an odd parity and can be derived by the reduction exclusive-OR of the data. The even flag is set high if the least significant bit of the data is zero. The zero flag is set high if all the bits of the data are logically low, and this flag is obtained by negating the reduction-OR of the data.

In this section we will show how to model memory elements such as a random-access memory, a content-addressable memory, and a

```verilog
module barrel_shifter (in, direction, type, count,
                result, Nflag, Pflag, Eflag, Zflag);

input   [31:0]  in;      // input operand
input   direction;       // left or right
input   type;            // shift or rotate
input   [3:0]   count;   // shift count
output  [31:0]  result;  // result operand
output  Nflag, Pflag, Eflag, Zflag;

parameter LEFT   = 0 ,
          RIGHT  = 1 ,
          SHIFT  = 0 ,
          ROTATE = 1 ;

// Invoke the shift/rotate functions
// to obtain the result.

wire [31:0] result = (type === ROTATE) ?
        (rotate(in , count, direction)) :
        (shift (in , count, direction)) ;

// This function implements the SHF instruction
function [31:0] shift;

  input   [31:0]  in;
  input   [3:0]   count;
  input   direction;

  begin
    shift = (direction === RIGHT) ?
        (in >> count) : (in << count);
  end

endfunction                          continued
```

```
// This function implements the ROT instruction
function [31:0] rotate;

  input  [31:0] in;
  input  [3:0]  count;
  input  direction;

  reg    [31:0] reg_rotate;
  reg    t;
  integer i;

  begin
    reg_rotate = in[31:0];
    if (direction === RIGHT)
      for (i = 0; i < count; i = i + 1) begin
        t = reg_rotate[0];
        reg_rotate[30:0] = reg_rotate[31:1];
        reg_rotate[31] = t;
      end
    else if(direction === LEFT)
      for (i = 0; i < count; i = i + 1) begin
        t = reg_rotate[31];
        reg_rotate[31:1] = reg_rotate[30:0];
        reg_rotate[0] = t;
      end
    rotate = reg_rotate;
  end
  endfunction

  //  set condition codes -- remaining flags
  set_flags U3(result,Nflag,Pflag,Eflag,Zflag);

endmodule
```

Figure 4.7 Model of the barrel-shifter

```
module multiplier (operand1,operand2,result,
        Cflag, Pflag, Eflag, Zflag, Nflag);

  input  [15:0] operand1, operand2;
  output [31:0] result;
  output Cflag, Pflag, Eflag, Zflag, Nflag;

  assign {Cflag,result} = operand1 * operand2;

  set_flags  U2 (result,Nflag,Pflag,Eflag,Zflag);

endmodule
```

Figure 4.8 Model of the multiplier

```
module set_flags (value,
                  Nflag, Pflag, Eflag, Zflag);

   input   [31:0] value;
   output  Nflag, Pflag, Eflag, Zflag;

   wire    Nflag = value[31];
   wire    Pflag = ^(value[31:0]);      want odd parity
   wire    Eflag = ~value[0];
   wire    Zflag = ~(|(value[31:0]));

endmodule
```

Figure 4.9 Model for setting condition codes

register file. The latter is not used in our processor design but is provided here as an example.

Memories

Random-Access Memory

Read/write operations on the random-access memory (RAM) are controlled by the clock phases. In a two-phase design, one phase is used for the read cycle and the other is used for the write cycle.

Figure 4.10 shows the model for the RAM used in the SISC processor design. The write cycle of the RAM is controlled by the ph2 clock and the write enable signal wrenable. The do_write block is set to trigger when either of the two signals change. We assume that the address or data can change anytime during the phase as long as these signals maintain a setup time before the trailing edge of the phase clock. Hence, these signals are included as triggers for the do_write block. In the model of RAM, the read is a continuous assignment where the output data register is assigned the value of the data at the address currently on the address bus, as long as the phase ph1 is true.

The read and write phases can be switched depending on the design requirements. The data needs to be valid only for a predefined setup time. This is illustrated by defining setup in the module definition of the RAM. The access time is modeled as a read-delay to the output.

```
module ram (ph1, ph2, addr,
            wrenable, datain, dataout);

  parameter  WORDS       = 4095 ,
             SETUP       = 1 ,
             ACCESS_TIME = 5 ;

  input  ph1, ph2, wrenable;
  input  [11:0] addr;     // address bus
  input  [31:0] datain;   // input data bus
  output [31:0] dataout;  // output data bus

  // Define RAM as a register array
  reg    [31:0] ram_data[WORDS:0];

  // Read cycle
  wire   [31:0] # ACCESS_TIME
  dataout = (ph1 === 1) ?
            ram_data[addr[11:0]] : 32'hz;

  // Write cycle
  always @(posedge ph2 or addr or
          datain or wrenable) begin : do_write
    if (ph2 === 1 && wrenable === 1)
      ram_data[addr[11:0]] = #SETUP datain;
  end

endmodule
```

Figure 4.10   Model of the RAM

Content-Addressable Memory

In processor designs, content-addressable memories (CAMs) are
frequently used to perform parallel search and comparison operations.
However, CAMs need more logic in their design than RAMs, giving rise
to increased area and higher cost. Our SISC processor does not use any
CAM.

The RAM model ofFigure 4.10 can be modified to perform CAM-
like operations by using comparison functions as illustrated in Figure
4.11. The resulting output can be synchronized to one of the phase clocks
as needed.

```
module cam_ram (comparand,mask,result,.....);

. . . . . . . . . . . . . . . . . . . . .

output [WORDS:0] result;
input  [31:0] comparand, mask;
reg    [31:0] comparand, mask;
reg    [31:0] ram_data[WORDS:0];
                  // CAM as a register array

// associative operation

wire [WORDS:0] result =
  {((cam_data[WORDS] & mask) === comparand) ?
                          1'h1 : 1'h0,
   ((cam_data[WORDS-1] & mask) === comparand) ?
                          1'h1 : 1'h0,
   . . . . . . . . . . . . . . . .
   . . . . . . . . . . . . . . . .

((cam_data[0] & mask) === comparand) ?
                      1'h1 : 1'h0};
. . . . . . . . . . . . . . . .
. . . . . . . . . . . . . . . .

endmodule
```

Figure 4.11   Model of a CAM

Register File

The SISC processor uses a set of sixteen general-purpose
registers. The architecture of the processor requires two read operations
on the registers in a cycle but only one write operation. This implies that
the register set can be modeled as a multiport RAM.

The model of a register file with two read ports and one write port
is shown in Figure 4.12. As in the model of the RAM, the read and write
cycles consist of two loops executing in parallel, one loop for read and
one loop for write. During the read cycle, the dataout output registers get
the value in the RAM at the address determined by the two address buses.
The address bus Aaddr is also used during the write cycle and is
multiplexed by the write enable signal.

```
module reg_file (ph1, ph2, Aaddr, Baddr,
        wrenable, datain, Adataout, Bdataout);

input   ph1, ph2;  // clock phases
input   wrenable;  // write-enable
input   [3:0]  Aaddr, Baddr; // address
input   [31:0] datain;       // input data
output  [31:0] Adataout, Bdataout;
                       // output data buses
reg     [31:0] Adataout, Bdataout;
                       // holds data values
reg     [31:0] ram_data[15:0];
                       // RAM as a register array

parameter   SETUP       = 1 ,
            ACCESS_TIME = 5 ;

// read cycle
always @(posedge ph1 or Aaddr or
                     Baddr or wrenable)
if (ph1 === 1 && wrenable === 0) begin
  # ACCESS_TIME
  Adataout = ram_data[Aaddr[3:0]];
  Bdataout = ram_data[Baddr[3:0]];
end

// write cycle
always @(posedge ph2 or Aaddr or
                 datain or wrenable)
if (ph2 === 1 && wrenable === 1)
  ram_data[Aaddr[11:0]] = #SETUP datain;

endmodule
```

Figure 4.12 Model of the register file

Clock Generator

The clock signal synchronizes events in different parts of the circuit and, in particular, synchronizes the updating of memory elements, such as flip-flops and latches. In most cases the master clock is generated outside the VLSI chip. The on-chip clock generator is coupled to the master clock through a phase-locked loop which provides stability to the clock by compensating for variations in the duty cycle. Although our processor uses a two-phase clock, we will present models for both single- and two-phase clocks.

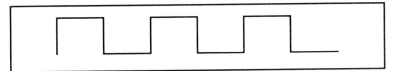

Figure 4.13 A 50% duty cycle clock

Single-Phase Clock

The simplest clock model generates a single 50% duty cycle as shown in Figure 4.13.

Figure 4.14 describes the model for the simple clock generator. It defines a register, masterclk, which switches state from 1 to 0 and from 0 to 1 at a given frequency. The period of the clock depends on the design and is user defined. A more general clock generator has a variable duty cycle.

```
module clock_gen (masterclk);

  parameter MASTERCLK_PERIOD = 10 ;

  output masterclk;
  reg    masterclk;

  initial
    masterclk = 0;

  // oscillation at a given period
  always begin
    # MASTERCLK_PERIOD/2
    masterclk = ~masterclk;
  end

endmodule
```

Figure 4.14 Model of the 50% duty cycle clock

Two-Phase Clock

While the clock generator of Figure 4.15 is sufficient for single-phase designs, most current processors are based on two-phase clocks. In this scheme, the basic memory element is a transparent latch whose output follows its input as long as the clock is high but stays latched when the cycle goes low.

In a two-phase clock design, some latches are clocked by phase-1 of the clock, and some are clocked by phase-2. Usually the two types of latches alternate; the output of phase-1 latches feed (possibly through some combinational logic) the data input of phase-2 latches, and vice versa.

Figure 4.15 shows a two-phase, nonoverlapping clock.

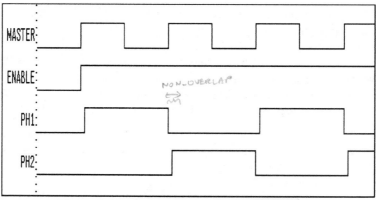

Figure 4.15   A two-phase, nonoverlapping clock

Figure 4.16 provides a model for generating a two-phase clock. The phase clocks are one-half the frequency of the master clock and are synchronized to the leading edge of the master clock. The phase generator produces two-phase, nonoverlapping clocks at one-half the frequency of the master clock.

In the phase generator module, phase_gen, a reset mechanism is provided in which the phase clocks are shut down if the enable signal is low for two consecutive rising edges of the master clock. Figure 4.17 shows the waveforms obtained by combining the two models together and running them as one clock unit.

```
module phase_gen (masterclk,enable,ph1,ph2);

parameter NON_OVERLAP = 1 ;

input    masterclk, enable;
output   ph1, ph2;
reg      ph1, ph2, reset;

initial begin // reset all signals
  ph1 = 0;
  ph2 = 0;
  reset = 0;
end

always @(posedge masterclk) begin : generate_phases
  if (enable == 1) begin
    ph2 = 0;
    # NON_OVERLAP
    ph1 = 1;
    @(posedge masterclk) begin
      ph1 = 0;
      # NON_OVERLAP;
      ph2 = 1;
    end
  end
end

always @(posedge masterclk) begin
  if (enable == 0) begin
    reset = 1;
    @(posedge masterclk) begin
      if (enable === 0 && reset === 1) begin
        ph1 = 0;
        ph2 = 0;
        reset = 0;
      end else
        reset = 0;
    end
  end
end

endmodule
```

how long ?

2 consecutive rising edge

Figure 4.16 Model of the two-phase clock generator

Clock Driver

The clock_driver module invokes the clock_gen and phase_gen modules to create a two-phase, nonoverlapping clock waveform, which is shown in Figure 4.18.

81

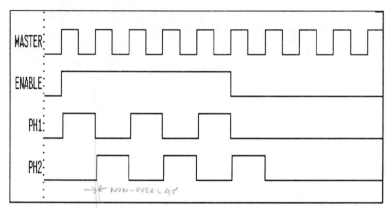

Figure 4.17 Output of the two-phase clock generator

```
module clock_driver;

reg enable;

clock_gen P1(master);
phase_gen P2(master, enable, ph1, ph2);

initial begin
  enable = 0;
  #10 enable = 1;
  #100 enable = 0;
  #100
  $stop;
end

initial begin
  $gr_waves("MASTER", master,
  "ENABLE", P2.enable,
  "PH1", P2.ph1,
  "PH2", P2.ph2);
end

endmodule
```

Figure 4.18 Driver for the clock generator

Control Unit

The control unit coordinates the operations among the various functional blocks of the processor. Figure 4.19 gives the equations of all the control lines for the nonpipelined processor. Similar equations can be developed for the pipelined version.

The output of each control signal depends on the state of the processor. The processor goes through three states—fetch, execute, and write—in sequence for each instruction.

The memory read-write signal, m_rw, is a write signal only if the state is write and the instruction opcode is a write. During the fetch cycle,

```
module control_pla (pc_dataout, pc_datain, pc_cmd,
      ir_datain, ir_cmd, ir_dataout, rf_write,
      rf_dataw, rf_addrw, rf_data1, rf_addr1,
      rf_data2, rf_addr2, alu_function,alu_src1,
      alu_src2, alu_result, psr_datain, psr_cmd,
      psr_dataout, m_data, m_addr, m_rw_ , state);

'define      NOP        4'h0
'define      BRA        4'h1
'define      LOAD       4'h2
'define      STORE      4'h3
'define      ADD        4'h4
'define      MUL        4'h5
'define      CMP        4'h6
'define      SHF        4'h7
'define      ROT        4'h8
'define      HALT       4'h9
'define      FETCH      2'h1
'define      EXECUTE    2'h2
'define      WRITE      2'h3

input   [11:0] pc_dataout;
input   [1:0]  state;
input   [4:0]  psr_dataout;
input   [31:0] ir_dataout, rf_data1, rf_data2;
input   [32:0] alu_result;
inout   [31:0] m_data;
reg     [31:0] m_data_reg;
output         rf_write, m_rw_;
output  [1:0]  pc_cmd, ir_cmd, psr_cmd;
output  [3:0]  rf_addrw, rf_addr1, rf_addr2, alu_function;
output  [4:0]  psr_datain;
output  [11:0] pc_datain, m_addr;
output  [31:0] ir_datain, rf_dataw, alu_src1, alu_src2;
'define      CLEAR_REG    2'h0
'define      HOLD_VAL     2'h1
'define      LOAD_REG     2'h2
'define      COUNTUP      2'h3
'define      IR_OPCODE    ir_dataout[31:28]
'define      IR_SRC_TYP   ir_dataout[27]
'define      IR_DST_TYP   ir_dataout[26]
'define      IR_SRC       ir_dataout[23:12]
'define      IR_SRC_REG   ir_dataout[15:12]
'define      IR_DST       ir_dataout[11:0]
'define      IR_DST_REG   ir_dataout[3:0]
'define      IMMEDIATE    1
```

```
`define      MEM_READ    1
`define      MEM_WRITE   0
`define      REG_READ    0
`define      REG_WRITE   1
`define      IR_CCODES   ir_dataout[27:23]

wire [31:0] m_data = m_data_reg;
wire m_rw_ = (`IR_OPCODE === `STORE && state === `WRITE) ?
             `MEM_WRITE : `MEM_READ;
wire [11:0] m_addr = (state === `FETCH) ? pc_dataout :
             ((`IR_OPCODE === `STORE) ? `IR_DST : `IR_SRC);

always @ (state) begin
   if(state === `EXECUTE || state === `WRITE) begin
      if(`IR_OPCODE === `STORE && `IR_SRC_TYP != `IMMEDIATE)
         m_data_reg = rf_data1;
      else
         if(`IR_OPCODE === `STORE && `IR_SRC_TYP === `IMMEDIATE)
            m_data_reg = `IR_SRC ;
         else m_data_reg = 32'hz;
   end
   else
      m_data_reg = 32'hz;
end

wire [3:0] alu_function =
      (`IR_OPCODE >= `ADD &&
       `IR_OPCODE <= `ROT &&
       state === `EXECUTE)  ? `IR_OPCODE : `NOP;
wire [31:0] alu_src1 = (`IR_SRC_TYP != `IMMEDIATE) ?
      ((`IR_OPCODE != `ROT &&
        `IR_OPCODE != `SHF) ? rf_data1 : `IR_SRC) : `IR_SRC;
wire [31:0] alu_src2 = rf_data2;
wire [3:0]  rf_addr1 = `IR_SRC_REG ;
wire [3:0]  rf_addr2 = `IR_DST_REG ;
wire [3:0]  rf_addrw = `IR_DST_REG ;
wire rf_write = (`IR_OPCODE != `BRA &&
         `IR_OPCODE != `STORE &&
         `IR_OPCODE != `NOP &&
         `IR_OPCODE != `HALT &&
          state === `WRITE) ? `REG_WRITE : `REG_READ;
wire [31:0] rf_dataw =
         (rf_write &&
         `IR_OPCODE === `LOAD &&
         `IR_SRC_TYP != `IMMEDIATE) ? m_data :
         ((rf_write && `IR_OPCODE === `LOAD &&
         `IR_SRC_TYP === `IMMEDIATE) ? `IR_SRC : alu_result);
wire [1:0] ir_cmd = (state === `FETCH) ?
         `LOAD_REG : ((state === `EXECUTE) ? `HOLD_VAL :
         ((`IR_OPCODE === `HALT) ? `CLEAR_REG : `HOLD_VAL));
wire [31:0] ir_datain = (ir_cmd === `LOAD_REG) ?
         m_data : ((ir_cmd === `CLEAR_REG) ?
         32'h0 : ir_dataout);
wire branch_taken = | ( `IR_CCODES & psr_dataout);
wire [1:0] pc_cmd = (state === `WRITE) ?
         ((`IR_OPCODE === `HALT) ?
```

```
            `CLEAR_REG : (branch_taken ?
            `LOAD_REG : `COUNTUP)) : `HOLD_VAL;
wire [11:0] pc_datain = (state == `WRITE) ?
            ((`IR_OPCODE == `HALT) ? 12'h0 : (branch_taken ?
            `IR_DST : (pc_dataout + 1))) : pc_dataout;
wire [1:0] psr_cmd = (`IR_OPCODE >= `ADD &&
            `IR_OPCODE <= `ROT &&
            state === `WRITE) ? `LOAD_REG :
            ((`IR_OPCODE === `HALT) ? `CLEAR_REG : `HOLD_VAL) ;
wire zflag = ~(|alu_result[31:0]);
wire eflag = ~(alu_result[0]);
wire pflag = ^(alu_result[31:0]);
wire [4:0] psr_datain = (psr_cmd === `CLEAR_REG) ? 5'h0
            ((psr_cmd === `LOAD_REG) ?
            {alu_result[31], zflag, pflag, eflag, alu_result[32]}
            : psr_dataout);

endmodule
```

Figure 4.19 Model of the control-unit PLA

the memory address m_addr is set to the program counter in order to fetch the next instruction. During the other states, m_addr gets its value from the instruction register source or destination fields.

The memory data bus, m_data, is a bidirectional bus which gets its value from m_data_reg. In fetch state, m_data acts as an input and, therefore, m_data_reg is tristated. In nonfetch state, if the opcode is a store, the register gets its value from either the register file or the instruction register depending on the type of the instruction.

In execute state, the alu_function signal is taken from the operand field of the IR, while the operands are taken from the register file or from the IR (for an immediate operand).

The data input to the register file is normally taken from the output of the ALU. The only exception is during execution of a load instruction. In that case, the input to the register file comes from the instruction register for immediate instruction or from the memory data register for nonimmediate instruction.

The operation of the program counter, the instruction register, and the status register depends on their respective command registers (pc_cmd, ir_cmd, and psr_cmd). During a given state, a command register can instruct a register to retain its value, to load a new value in, to increment its value, or to clear the register. In the fetch state, the instruction register is updated with a new value from memory and maintains its value during all other states. The program counter increments its value at the end of every write state except when a branch occurs. The value of the status register depends on the output of the ALU and is derived as a function of alu_result. All three registers—PC, IR, and PSR—are cleared when the opcode is HLT.

The control block as described above models only the combinational part of the control block. The logic for generating the timing signals is not modeled. This logic has to implement a state machine to synchronize the updating of the control block state (IR, PC, and so forth) to the right processor state (fetch, execute, write) and to the right clock phase.

Summary

In this chapter we presented a structural model of the SISC, based upon its instruction set model from the previous chapter. Various building blocks of a computer and a central processor were modeled using the SISC as an example. The equations for the control unit of the CPU were also developed. These can be implemented using a PLA or some library components. These models can be used as guidelines to design more complex architectures.

CHAPTER

5

Modeling Cache Memories

A cache in a computer system stores data from the most frequently accessed addresses in a smaller, higher speed, local memory. This cache memory can be accessed faster than main memory; and, provided that the data in the cache is used more than once, the average access time required for memory transactions is reduced.

The cache is always small compared to main memory because cache RAMs are more expensive than the slower dynamic RAMs used for main memory. As a result, only a small portion of the main memory can be stored in the cache. The concept of caching is predicated upon the observed phenomenon that computer programs use only a small subset of memory at each point in time (the principle of locality). The efficiency of a cache is measured by the cache hit ratio, i.e., the number of times data is accessed from the cache over the total number of accesses. Typical hit ratios are in the range of from eighty to one hundred percent.

Data in a cache memory is like money in a cash register, and data in main memory is like money in the bank. Obtaining money from the bank can be quite a tedious task, but money in the cash register is easy to use. Money that is added to the cash register is not taken to the bank immediately since it may be required again shortly after.

In this chapter we examine the process of modeling a simple cache in Verilog. Complete code for a basic cache model appears at the end of this chapter in Figure 5.17. Even a simple cache improves the performance of a processor significantly. At the end of this chapter we also look at ways of improving the basic design; but first, let us examine how the cache will communicate with the environment around it.

Interfaces

A cache system typically lies between the processor and the main system bus. The following block diagram (Figure 5.1) describes the signals and buses that the cache needs to communicate with the processor and the system. Note that in our system the system bus is synonymous with main memory. The terms will be used interchangeably in the text.

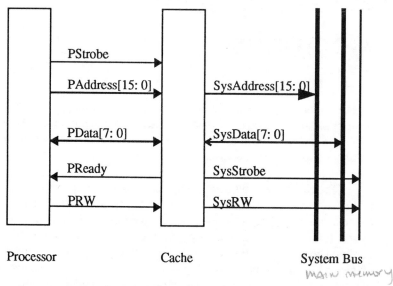

Figure 5.1 System block diagram

Processor Interface

The processor interface consists of the processor address bus, PAddress[15: 0], the processor data bus, PData[7: 0], and control signals PStrobe and PReady. The PStrobe is asserted when the processor is starting a bus transaction and a valid address is on the PAddress bus. PReady is used to signal to the processor that the bus transaction is completed. The timing diagram in Figure 5.2 demonstrates a simple read cycle. The PRW signal is high for a read and low for a write.

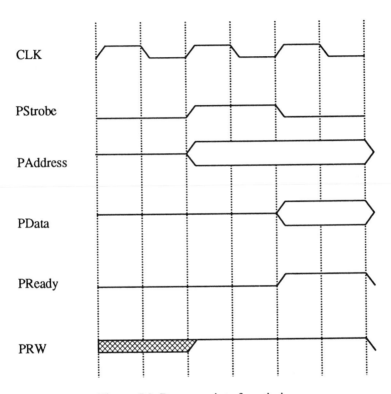

Figure 5.2 Processor interface timing

System Bus Interface

For our cache model we assume a simple bus model. For a read operation, the SysAddress is first presented to the bus along with the SysStrobe signal and the SysRW. The SysRW signal is high for read operations and low for write operations. After a set number of wait states, the data is returned. A write operation is similar, but the data is driven onto the PData bus immediately and then waits for the set number of wait states before issuing another write operation. Figure 5.3 shows a system read with one wait state.

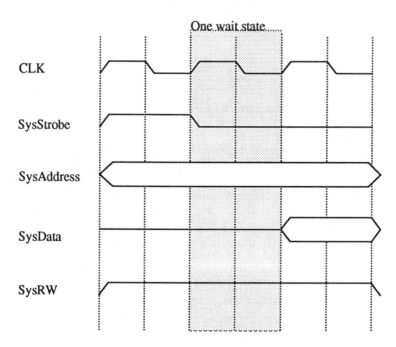

Figure 5.3 System interface timing

Cache Architecture

As this is not a book on cache architecture it suffices to implement a direct-mapped cache, the simplest of all cache architectures. A direct mapped cache consists of a single tag RAM, cache RAM, and a simple controller. We model each of these parts separately and then bring them together in the final model.

We will assume that the processor has a 16-bit address which gives it an address space of 64K bytes. With this in mind, a cache size of 1K bytes was chosen as a reasonable trade-off between cost and performance for this processor. The appropriate size for a cache is directly related to the hardware cost and to the required performance for the type of code to be run on the processor.

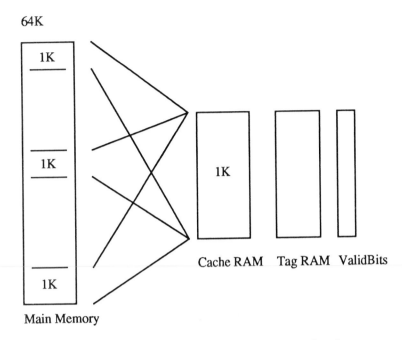

64K

Main Memory

Figure 5.4 Mapping between main memory and cache

The main memory is divided up into 64 blocks of 1K each. The mapping between the cache memory and the main memory is shown in Figure 5.4. Note that each location in the cache is mapped to 64 different locations in main memory. For example, locations 52, 1K+52, 2K+52, ... , 63K+52 in main memory, all map to location 52 in the cache. This means that only the least significant 10 bits of the address are needed to address the cache. In order to identify the full address of a cache entry, each cache entry has a 6-bit tag that matches the 6 most significant bits of the main memory address corresponding to the entry currently stored in that cache location. The 16-bit address is divided into index and tag fields as shown in Figure 5.5. In addition, each cache entry has a single bit that indicates whether the entry is valid. Initially, all entries are set to invalid.

To further simplify the cache, a write-through mode of operation is used. This means that all writes from the processor update both the cache and main memory. Thus the cache memory is always kept coherent with main memory. Further study into cache systems reveals many other

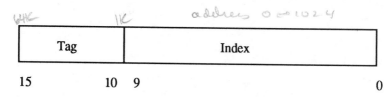

Figure 5.5 Address fields

write-back policies that improve performance incrementally and add to the complexity of the controller.

Block Diagram

The three major sections of the cache subsystem are shown in Figure 5.6.

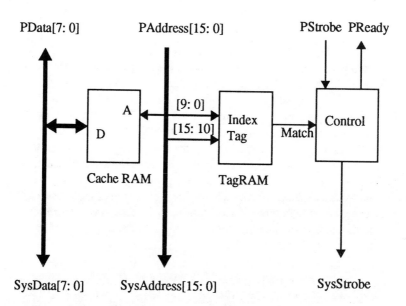

Figure 5.6 Cache subsystem block diagram

High Level Modeling

When writing a model at the highest level, it is important to abstract the most relevant features of the design and discard all the rest. This usually involves the extraction of the elements that contain the "state" of the system, modeling these as data structures, and then lumping all of the control into one piece of code. In this case the state of the cache is contained in the tag RAM and in the cache RAM. The data structures for tag and cache RAMs need to be defined. A real physical cache would also have latches, transceivers, and buffers; but these can be discarded from the high level model to simplify its implementation.

Tag RAM Model

The tag RAM model consists of a memory array capable of holding one tag for each index location, i.e., 1K x 6, and a memory array containing a single bit for each index location indicating whether that location contains valid data. Figure 5.7 shows how each valid bit corresponds to an entry in the Tag RAM.

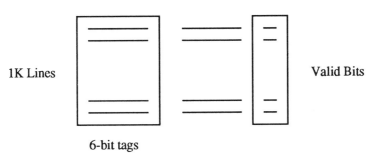

1K Lines   Valid Bits

6-bit tags

Figure 5.7 Tag RAM and valid bits

Figure 5.8 demonstrates the code used to implement the tag RAM model. Some useful constants are also defined at the same time.

Cache RAM Model

The cache RAM model is simply a memory array containing 8 bits of data for each of the index locations. It is addressed by the processor

93

```
// TagRAM Model
`define CACHESIZE 1024
`define INDEX 9:0
`define TAG 15:10
reg [`TAG] TagRam [`CACHESIZE-1:0];
reg [`CACHESIZE-1:0] ValidBits;
`define PRESENT 1
`define ABSENT ! `PRESENT


// Cache RAM Model
`define DATASIZE 8
reg [`DATASIZE-1:0] CacheRam [`CACHESIZE-1:0];
```

Figure 5.8 Code for tag RAM and cache RAM models

address, and its data is provided either from the processor or from the system bus. The code for the Cache RAM model is show in Figure 5.8.

Controller Model

Figure 5.9 shows a flow chart for the main code of the controller. Drawing high level flow charts can help you identify the sections of the model that must run in parallel and other sections that would be implemented better with simple code. The controller can have a single main loop, but we use a number of other parallel structures to take care of some details, such as asserting PReady and tristating the data buses at the appropriate times.

At the beginning, a loop waits for the processor to start a cycle with the assertion of PStrobe. This signal is sampled at the rising edge of the clock. If it is asserted, the address is looked up in the cache. If the tag that is stored in the tag RAM for this address matches the tag of the current processor address and the corresponding valid bit is set, then data for this address is stored in the cache. Based on whether the address hits in the cache and on the state of the PRW line, the correct sequence of

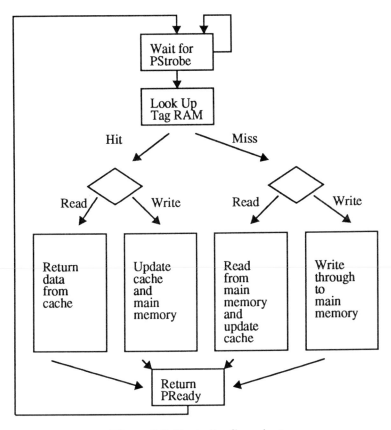

Figure 5.9 Controller flow chart

subsequent actions are determined. The four possibilities and their associated actions are

1. Read Hit, return data from cache.

2. Read Miss, fetch and return data from memory and update cache.

3. Write Hit, write to cache and to memory.

4. Write Miss, write to memory only.

95

Each of these cases is described in detail later in this chapter. Note that all transactions on the system bus take a set number of cycles regardless of the type of transaction. During each of the bus operations there is a loop that waits for those cycles to pass. The number of wait states, i.e., additional cycles, that the bus needs is defined as WAITSTATES. At the end of each bus transaction, the controller asserts PReady for one cycle to indicate to the processor that the transaction is finished.

To simplify the coding of the main part of the model, all of the operations that can happen in parallel are identified, and triggered by separate events. For example, the assertion of PReady actually requires two cycles because it must first be asserted high then deasserted low. The burden of keeping track of this is offloaded into a separate *always* loop and triggered by the event named SignalPReady. Other similar situations arise on the system side. The code for each of these cases is shown in Figure 5.10.

Verilog's parallelism does help significantly in the following:

- the SysStrobe signal must be deasserted after one clock cycle when a system transaction is started.

- the bus should be tristated at the end of a bus transaction.

- the Tag RAM and Cache RAMs can all be updated in parallel.

Although it is possible to write models without having the ability of running more than one piece of code in parallel, Verilog's constructs help in model abstraction and result in final code that better represents the physical implementation.

Read Hit

Of all the possible cache operations, read hits happen the most often because of the locality of bus references for typical software. In the cycle following the processor strobe, data is returned to the processor from the cache RAM along with the assertion of PReady. The code in Figure 5.11 demonstrates by its simplicity the advantage of having coded the parallel sections separately. Returning the data requires two clock edges, one to drive the data and then one to tristate the bus. Similarly,

```
event
 UpdateCacheRam,UpdateTagRam,SignalPReady,
 ReturnCacheData,ReturnSysData,StartSysRead,
 StartSysWrite,EndSysRead,EndSysWrite;
always @(UpdateCacheRam) begin
 CacheRam[PAddress['INDEX]]=PData; // update cache
 end
always @(UpdateTagRam) begin
 TagRam[PAddress['INDEX]]=PAddress['TAG]; //update tagram
 ValidBits[PAddress['INDEX]]='PRESENT;
 end
always @(SignalPReady) begin //Assert PReady for one cycle
 #1 PReady=1;
 @(posedge Clk) #1 PReady=0;
 end
always @(ReturnCacheData) begin
 // Return data to processor
 #1 PDataReg=CacheRam[PAddress['INDEX]];
 @(posedge Clk) #1 PDataReg='bz; //Turn off PData drivers
 end
always @(ReturnSysData) begin
 #1 PDataReg=SysData; // return data to processor
 @(posedge Clk) #1 PDataReg='bz; // Turn off PData
 end
always @(StartSysRead) begin
 #1
 SysAddress=PAddress;
 SysDataReg='bz;
 SysRW='READ;
 SysStrobe=1; // Access main memory
 @(posedge Clk) #1 SysStrobe=0;
 // wait for memory read
 for(i=0;i<'WAITSTATES;i=i+1) @(posedge Clk);
 -> EndSysRead;
 end
always @(StartSysWrite) begin
 #1
 SysAddress=PAddress;
 SysDataReg=PData;
 SysRW='WRITE;
 SysStrobe=1; // Access main memory
 // wait for memory update
 @(posedge Clk) #1 SysStrobe=0;
 for(i=0;i<'WAITSTATES;i=i+1) @(posedge Clk);
 -> EndSysWrite;
 @(posedge Clk) SysDataReg=8'bz;
 end
```

Figure 5.10 Parallel events

97

```
        begin
                -> ReturnCacheData;
                -> SignalPReady;
        end // READ Hit
```

Figure 5.11 Code for read hit

signaling PReady requires two cycles: one to activate PReady and one to deactivate it.

Write Hit

Since the cache protocol is write-through, both the cache and main memory must be updated. Main memory is updated at the same time to maintain cache coherency. This simply means that main memory always has a copy of the most recent data. A write cycle must be performed on the system bus at the same time that data is written to the cache. After the preset number of wait states, PReady is returned to the processor to indicate the completion of the transaction. The Tag RAM does not need modifying. Figure 5.12 shows the code for a write hit.

```
    begin // update cache and write-through to memory
        -> StartSysWrite;
        -> UpdateCacheRam;
        @(EndSysWrite) -> SignalPReady;
    end // WRITE Hit
```

Figure 5.12 Code for write hit

Read Miss

A read miss occurs if the location in the cache, corresponding to the current processor address, is either invalid or contains data for a different address. A memory cycle reads data from main memory. After the set number of wait states have passed, the data is available for writing into cache and for returning to the processor. At the same time, the Tag RAM is updated to reflect the tag of the new data and the valid bit is set.

Figure 5.13 shows the code that handles a read operation that missed in the cache.

```
begin
     -> StartSysRead;
     @ (EndSysRead)
          -> ReturnSysData;
          -> SignalPReady;
     @ (posedge Clk)
          -> UpdateCacheRam;
          -> UpdateTagRam;
end // READ miss
```

Figure 5.13 Code for Read Miss

Write Miss

In the case of a write miss, only main memory is updated. Analysis shows that for the type of code most likely to run on this type of processor this policy is preferable to updating the cache as well. The model performs a write to memory only and returns PReady when the bus transaction is complete. Figure 5.14 shows the actions necessary for a write miss.

```
begin
     -> StartSysWrite;
     @ (EndSysWrite) -> SignalPReady;
end // WRITE miss
```

Figure 5.14 Code for Write Miss

Testing

Testing the cache on its own requires writing a special driver to simulate processor operation. The code for the cache driver instantiates one copy of the cache model and includes tasks for read and write operations as if they had come from the processor. There is a simple model for main memory as well. At the end of the module, a short test first writes to a location, then reads from that location several times. The write operation writes through to memory without updating the cache, and the first read operation loads the cache with data for that address. The

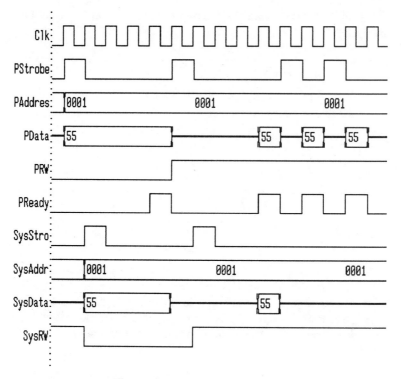

Figure 5.15 Result of Short Test

second read operation is a cache hit and is thus much faster than the first read.

The command used to run this test is

```
verilog cache.v cachedriver.v.
```

Figure 5.15 shows the waveforms generated by this short test.

The waveforms obtained from running the simulation demonstrate that the cache model works correctly. More stringent tests should be written to fully prove the functionality of the model. Given the provided tasks for reading and writing data, the task of fully testing the cache is reduced to a series of loops to check writing and reading all memory locations.

If trace data, i.e., address traces from running real programs on the processor were available, this model could be used for performance evaluations for the cache size and architecture chosen.

Performance Improvements

All real caching systems have the mechanisms demonstrated in the foregoing simple cache model. Some suggestions are offered here for improving the performance of the basic model for real world applications.

Two-Way Set Associativity

The simplest way to describe two-way set associativity is to say it is like having two direct-mapped caches similar to the one in the model. Both Tag RAMs are looked up simultaneously, and data is provided from the cache where an address generates a hit. The data cannot reside in both caches because it is never written into both caches. During a replacement, one of the caches receives the data, chosen either randomly or by a least-recently-used algorithm.

Multi-way set associativity relieves a problem called "thrashing". Thrashing occurs when a program accesses two different locations that map to the same location in the cache. A two-way set associative cache provides two places where one address can be mapped. The model remains almost the same, but the Tag and Cache RAMs are duplicated and a tag replacement strategy is implemented.

Higher associativities are simply extensions of this same principle and provide further improvements in performance. The actual improvement depends on the type of code and cache size.

Write Buffering

Write buffering is, in a way, a mechanism that enables the cache subsystem to "lie" to the processor about the completion of writes. As the cache controller starts a write on the system bus it returns ready immediately to the processor before the write completes. The processor then proceeds and, provided that it does not do a transaction that requires the system bus before the current write is completed, it gains valuable cycles. For example, if a write is followed by a read that hits in the cache, the

```
begin
    -> StartSysWrite;
    -> SignalPReady;
end // WRITE miss
```

Figure 5.16 Code for Write Buffering Version of Write Miss

read takes place while the write onto the system bus is still being completed.

To upgrade the model to allow for write buffering, the code for the write must be modified so that PReady is returned immediately after the system bus transaction begins. Figure 5.16 demonstrates how this can be accomplished.

Note that another system transaction cannot be started until the current one is completed. As the implementation stands, this actually happens if one write follows another. Note also that if a StartSysWrite event is signalled, it will not be processed until the loop from the previous write is completed. This does not, however, take care of the case where a system read follows a system write. Solve such a problem by combining the StartSysWrite and StartSysRead events into the same loop.

Larger Line Size

The line size is the number of words stored in the cache for each tag. In our simple example the line size is 1. In higher performance systems the line size can be much larger. Sometimes the system bus is capable of transferring the entire line during a single bus transaction. The number of words that the system bus can supply in one transaction is called the "block size". A larger block size improves bus performance by reducing the average overhead for bus accesses. Implementing a larger line size in our model simply means reducing the size of the Tag RAM. For example, if the line size were 4 words, a 1K cache would require only 256 tags. The Tag RAM would be indexed by PAddress[7:0]. To compensate for the reduced number of tags, each tag would then be 8 bits corresponding to PAddress[16:8]. As you can see, a larger block size can be implemented with a few almost trivial changes to the basic model.

If the bus is not capable of multi word transfers, a larger block size can still offer an advantage. During a cache miss, either the full block must be replaced one word at a time, or only the word that was requested is obtained and a valid bit is set. A valid bit is used for each word in the block indicating which words of the block are currently present in the cache. Larger block sizes in this case reduce the number of tags stored in the Tag RAM.

Write-Back Policy

Instead of always writing to memory, it is possible to write data back to memory only when a replacement would write over that location in the cache. An extra bit is required, along with the valid bit, for an indication of whether each location in the cache has been written to. Main memory is no longer coherent with the cache. Write-back caches are much more complicated than write-through caches, but they provide better performance in multi processor systems. Complexities arise in multi processor systems because of the difficulty in keeping multiple caches coherent with each other.

To upgrade the basic cache model to a write-back cache in our single processor system requires only the addition of the extra bit mentioned above to indicate modified lines. The code for the write hit case would change to just write into the cache and set the modified bit. The data would not be written through to the system bus until a replacement needed the same cache location.

Write-back caches are generally used in multi processing environments. The implementation of such a cache system is beyond the scope of the basic model and would require a number of additional signals on the system bus for maintaining coherency between multiple caches on the same bus.

Summary

The evaluation of alternatives is one of the main reasons for writing high level models. In this chapter a model of a direct-mapped cache was presented to demonstrate the versatility of Verilog as a high level modeling tool. This model or variations of it can be used to evaluate the performance of different cache architectures before any major design efforts have been started.

```
module cache(
        PStrobe,
        PAddress,
        PData,
        PRW,
        PReady,

        SysStrobe,
        SysAddress,
        SysData,
        SysRW,

        Clk
        );

input           PStrobe;
input   [15:0]  PAddress;
inout   [7:0]   PData;
input           PRW;
output          PReady;

output          SysStrobe;
output  [15:0]  SysAddress;
inout   [7:0]   SysData;
output          SysRW;

input           Clk;


`define READ 1
`define WRITE 0
`define CACHESIZE 1024
`define DATASIZE 8
`define ADDRESSSIZE 15
`define WAITSTATES 2 // wait states required for system
accesses

// Bidirectional Buses
reg     [`DATASIZE-1:0]    PDataReg;
wire    [`DATASIZE-1:0]    PData=PDataReg;
reg     [`DATASIZE-1:0]    SysDataReg;
wire    [`DATASIZE-1:0]    SysData=SysDataReg;
reg     [`ADDRESSSIZE-1:0] SysAddress;

// Control Signals
reg     PReady;
reg     SysStrobe;
reg     SysRW;
integer i;

// TagRam Model
`define INDEX 9:0
`define TAG 15:10
reg     [`TAG]  TagRam  [`CACHESIZE-1:0];
reg     [`CACHESIZE-1:0] ValidBits;
`define PRESENT 1
```

105

```
`define ABSENT ! `PRESENT

// Cache Ram Model
reg     [`DATASIZE-1:0]    CacheRam [`CACHESIZE-1:0];

event
    UpdateCacheRam,
    UpdateTagRam,
    SignalPReady,
    ReturnCacheData,
    ReturnSysData,
    StartSysRead,
    StartSysWrite,
    EndSysRead,
    EndSysWrite;

always @(UpdateCacheRam) begin
        CacheRam[PAddress[`INDEX]]=PData; // update cache
        end

always @(UpdateTagRam) begin
        // update tagram
        TagRam[PAddress[`INDEX]]=PAddress[`TAG];
        ValidBits[PAddress[`INDEX]]=`PRESENT;
        end

always @(SignalPReady) begin // Assert PReady for one cycle
        #1 PReady=1;
        @(posedge Clk) #1 PReady=0;
        end

always @(ReturnCacheData) begin
        // Return data to processor
        #1 PDataReg=CacheRam[PAddress[`INDEX]];
        @(posedge Clk)
        #1 PDataReg='bz; // Turn off PData drivers
        end

always @(ReturnSysData) begin
        #1 PDataReg=SysData; // return data to processor
        @(posedge Clk)
        #1 PDataReg='bz; // Turn off PData drivers
        end

always @(StartSysRead) begin
        #1
        SysAddress=PAddress;
        SysDataReg='bz;
        SysRW=`READ;
        SysStrobe=1; // Access main memory
        @(posedge Clk) #1 SysStrobe=0;
        // wait for memory read
        for(i=0;i<`WAITSTATES;i=i+1) @(posedge Clk);
        -> EndSysRead;
        end
```

```
always @(StartSysWrite) begin
       #1
       SysAddress=PAddress;
       SysDataReg=PData;
       SysRW='WRITE;
       SysStrobe=1; // Access main memory
       // wait for memory update
       @(posedge Clk) #1 SysStrobe=0;
       for(i=0;i<'WAITSTATES;i=i+1) @(posedge Clk);
       -> EndSysWrite;
       @(posedge Clk) SysDataReg=8'bz;
       end


   // Controller
   always @(posedge Clk) if(PStrobe) begin
       // processor starting access
       if((TagRam[PAddress['INDEX]]==PAddress['TAG])&&
           ValidBits[PAddress['INDEX]])
           // Address hits in cache
           if(PRW=='READ) // READ Hit
              begin
                 $display("ReadHit");
                 -> ReturnCacheData;
                 -> SignalPReady;
              end // READ Hit
           else // WRITE Hit
              begin //update cache and write through
                 $display("WriteHit");
                 -> StartSysWrite;
                 -> UpdateCacheRam;
                 @(EndSysWrite) -> SignalPReady;
              end // WRITE Hit
       else // Address misses in cache
           if(PRW=='READ) // READ miss
              begin
                 $display("ReadMiss");
                 -> StartSysRead;
                 @(EndSysRead)
                 -> ReturnSysData;
                 -> SignalPReady;
                 @(posedge Clk)
                 -> UpdateCacheRam;
                 -> UpdateTagRam;
              end // READ miss
           else // WRITE miss (update memory only)
              begin
                 $display("WriteMiss");
                 -> StartSysWrite;
                 @(EndSysWrite) -> SignalPReady;
              end // WRITE miss
       end
```

```
initial begin
        // initialize tagram
        for(i=0;i<'CACHESIZE;i=i+1)
                ValidBits[i]='ABSENT;
        PDataReg=8'bz;
        SysDataReg=8'bz;
        SysAddress=0;
        SysStrobe=0;
        SysRW=1;
        PReady=0;
        end

endmodule


module cachedriver();

'define MemorySize 64*1024

reg                PStrobe;
reg        [15:0]  PAddress;
reg        [7:0]   PDataReg;
wire       [7:0]   PData=PDataReg;
reg                PRW;

wire               SysStrobe;
wire       [15:0]  SysAddress;
reg        [7:0]   SysDataReg;
wire       [7:0]   SysData=SysDataReg;
wire               SysRW;

reg                Clk;

reg[7:0]MainMemory ['MemorySize-1:0];

cache cache(
        .PStrobe (PStrobe),
        .PAddress (PAddress),
        .PData (PData),
        .PRW (PRW),
        .PReady (PReady),

        .SysStrobe (SysStrobe),
        .SysAddress (SysAddress),
        .SysData (SysData),
        .SysRW (SysRW),

        .Clk (Clk)
        );

initial begin
        PStrobe=0;
        PAddress=0;
        PDataReg=8'bz;
        PRW=0;
        SysDataReg=8'bz;
```

```
          Clk=0;
          end

always    begin // model of main system clock
          #10 Clk=1;
          #10 Clk=0;
          end

integer i;
always    // simple model of memory
          // wait for start of memory transaction
          @(posedge Clk) if(SysStrobe)
            if(SysRW=='READ) begin // read
              for(i=0;i<'WAITSTATES;i=i+1) @(posedge Clk);
              // Wait before returning data
              #1 // Return data
                SysDataReg=MainMemory[SysAddress];
              @(posedge Clk) #1
                SysDataReg=8'bz;
            end // read
            else begin // write
              for(i=0;i<'WAITSTATES;i=i+1) @(posedge Clk);
              MainMemory[SysAddress]=SysData;
            end // write

// Tasks used for writing test vectors
task PWrite;
input   [15:0]  Address;
input   [7:0]   Data;
begin
        #1
           PStrobe=1;
           PAddress=Address;
           PDataReg=Data;
        @(posedge Clk) #1
           PStrobe=0;
        @(posedge Clk)
           // wait till cache and memory
           // have finished transaction
           while(!PReady) @(posedge Clk);
        $display
           ("PWrite: Wrote %h to address %h",PData,PAddress);
end
endtask // PWrite

task PRead;
input   [15:0]  Address;
begin
        #1
           PStrobe=1;
           PRW='READ;
           PAddress=Address;
           PDataReg=8'bz;
        @(posedge Clk) #1
           PStrobe=0;
        // wait till cache and memory
```

```
        // have finished transaction
        @(posedge Clk) while(!PReady) @(posedge Clk);
        $display("PRead: read %h from address %h",
            PData,PAddress);
end
endtask // PRead

initial begin
            $gr_waves(
                "Clk", Clk,

                "PStrobe", PStrobe,
                "PAddress", PAddress,
                "PData", PData,
                "PRW", PRW,
                "PReady", PReady,

                "SysStrobe", SysStrobe,
                "SysAddress", SysAddress,
                "SysData", SysData,
                "SysRW", SysRW
            );

        @(posedge Clk)
                PWrite(1,'h55);
                PRead(1);
                PRead(1);
                PRead(1);
        #50 $stop;
        end
endmodule // cachedriver
```

Figure 5.17   Complete code for cache model

C H A P T E R

6

Modeling Asynchronous I/O: UART

In this chapter we present an example of modeling an asynchronous peripheral device, a dual Universal Asynchronous Receiver Transmitter (UART) chip. We develop two models of the chip. The first model is a high-level abstraction which describes the functionality of the chip and emphasizes simplicity, readability, and ease of change. The second model is oriented toward gate-level implementation. This model is partitioned so that a logic synthesizer can be used to automatically implement the chip with library components.

Functional Description of UART

A UART is used for communicating with serial input/output devices. Serial communication is needed either when the device is inherently serial (e.g. modems and telephone lines) or when the cabling cost has to be reduced at the expense of operating speed (e.g., a twisted pair in laboratory instrumentation).

Typically, the UART is connected between a central processor and a serial device. To the processor, the UART appears as an 8-bit parallel port which can be read from or written to. To the serial device, the UART presents two data wires, one for input and one for output, which serially

111

communicate 8-bit data. The rate of data communication depends on the peripheral device. Some devices operate at a single clock speed (e.g., old teletypes at 110 baud), and they generate the clock internally. Other devices can operate at multiple clock rates and get clock input from the UART.

To detect the start of a transmitted byte on the serial line, the line is held high between successive transmissions and is pulled low for a one-bit duration. Other issues relating to serial communications—such as parity, overruns, and stop bits—are not covered in this example.

Figure 6.2 shows a block diagram of the dual UART chip. It has two identical single UART modules which operate independently of each other. All the input/output pins of the chip are listed in Figure 6.1.

```
Signal name      Signal description      I/O
--------------------------------------------
reset            reset                   I
clkin            external clock          I
rd_              read signal             I
wr_              write signal            I
cs_0, cs_1       chip selects            I
din0, din1       serial data input       I
a[2:0]           address bus             I
dbus[7:0]        bidirectional data bus  I/O
int0, int1       interrupt lines         O
dout0, dout1     serial data outputs     O
clko0, clko1     output clocks           O
```

Figure 6.1 I/O pins of the UART chip

Each UART module has eight 8-bit registers for control and status. The registers can be read from and written to using the rd_ and wr_ signals. The a input is an address to select one of the eight registers to read or write. To improve the readability of the model, the register addresses have been assigned mnemonics. For example, address 0, which is the location of the transmit data register, is designated as XMITDT_ADDR. Figure 6.3 shows the mnemonics of the various addresses.

Waveforms for reading from and writing to an internal register are shown in Figure 6.4 and Figure 6.5.

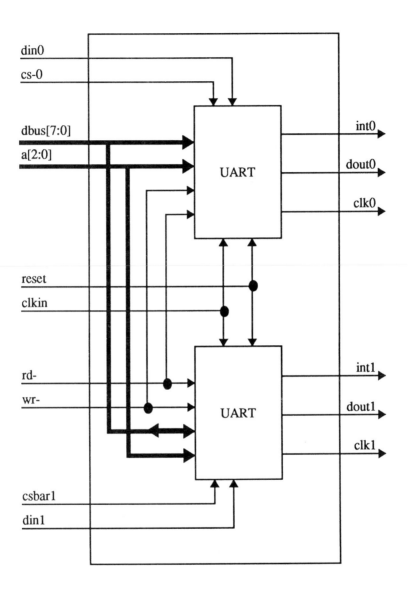

Figure 6.2 The dual UART Chip

113

```
        // The addresses of the internal registers
        parameter
                XMITDT_ADDR = 0,
                STATUS_ADDR = 1,
                DIVLSB_ADDR = 2,
                DIVMSB_ADDR = 3,
                RECVDT_ADDR = 4,
                CLRINT_ADDR = 7;
```

Figure 6.3 Register address mnemonics

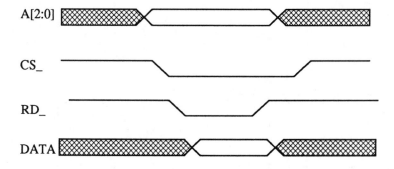

Figure 6.4 Reading from an internal register

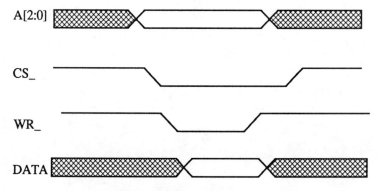

Figure 6.5 Writing to an internal register

Serial transmission is initiated when the host processor writes to register XMITDT of the UART. Reception is triggered by a falling edge of the serial data line (din). While transmitting or receiving, register STATUS reflects the current status. When either the transmission or the reception is complete, an interrupt is generated. The interrupt is cleared when register CLRINT of the corresponding UART is read. The status indicates the source of the interrupt (receive or transmit).

Registers DIVMSB and DIVLSB contain the most- and least-significant bits of a 16-bit integer, which divides the external clock to get the desired baud rate. Registers RECVDT and XMITDT contain the receive and transmit data. The rest of the registers in the register file are not used in this model; however, in a more complex design, they can hold other parameters such as parity, number of stop bits, overflow, and so forth.

Figure 6.6 shows the top-level structural model of the dual UART chip. It instantiates two single UART modules and follows the block diagram closely.

```
module dual_uart (
    dbus, a, reset, rd_, wr_,
    cs_0, cs_1, din0, din1, clkin,
    int0, int1, dout0, dout1, clko0, clko1
);
inout[7:0] dbus;
input[2:0] a;
input reset, rd_, wr_;
input cs_0, cs_1, din0, din1, clkin;

output int0, int1, dout0, dout1, clko0, clko1;

// The first instance of a single UART module
uart u0 (
    reset, dbus, a, rd_, wr_, cs_0, din0, clkin,
    int0, dout0, clko0
);

// The second instance of a single UART module
uart u1 (
    reset, dbus, a, rd_, wr_, cs_1, din1, clkin,
    int1, dout1, clko1
);
endmodule
```

Figure 6.6 Structural model of the dual UART

The next few sections describe the model of the single UART module.

Functional Model of the Single UART

In the functional model, we are concerned with the ease of modeling, readability, and maintainability. We disregard any implementation details. We use an array of registers to describe the internal status and control registers of the chip, which are convenient to program but might not be efficient to implement. We also use events and triggers, constructs which are difficult to synthesize. The functional model is shown schematically in Figure 6.8.

```
always @(negedge reset) begin : reset_block
    integer i;

    disable receive_block;
    disable transmit_block;
    oclkreg = 0;
    iclkreg = 0;
    int = 0;
    dbus_reg = 8'hzz;
    for (i = 0; i < 8; i = i + 1)
        regfile[i] = 0;
end
```

Figure 6.7 Reset operation

In the next sections we describe the main blocks in the model: the reset block, the clock generator, the read block, the write block, the transmit block and the receive block.

Reset Operation

Reset is initiated when the reset signal makes a negative transition. On reset, the model disables the receive and transmit blocks, initializes the clocks, sets all the registers in the register file to 0, and tristates the outputs. The code is shown in Figure 6.7.

Clock Generator

The UART generates both the transmit clock and the receive clock. The two clocks have the same frequency but may be shifted in phase with respect to each other. The external clock is divided by the

116

```
module uart (
    reset, dbus, a, rd_, wr_, cs_, din, clkin,
    int, dout, clko
);
// Input/output declarations
...

// The addresses of the internal registers
parameter ...

// The internal state
parameter
    TRANSMITTING = 0,
    RECEIVING = 1,
    DONE_XMT = 2,
    DONE_RCV = 3;

reg[7:0] regfile [0:7];
wire[15:0] divisor =
  { regfile[DIVMSB_ADDR], regfile[DIVLSB_ADDR] };
reg[15:0] oclkreg, iclkreg;
reg xmt_clock, rcv_clock;
event do_transmit;

integer lines;

initial begin
    lines = 0;
    oclkreg = 0;
    iclkreg = 0;
    $monitor
("%m:r[0]=%h,r[1]=%h,r[2]=%h,r[3]=%h,r[4]=%h,time=%0d",
regfile[0],regfile[1],regfile[2],regfile[3],regfile[4],$time);
  end

// All the functional blocks of the module
// are described in the following subsection

// Reset operation
...
// Clock generator
...
// Read operation
...
// Write operation
...
// Transmit operation
...
// Receive operation
...
endmodule // single_uart
```

Figure 6.8 Functional model of the single UART

divisor, which is the concatenation of DIVMSB and DIVLSB. The receive and transmit clocks are generated in parallel, using the fork construct of Verilog as shown in Figure 6.9.

```
always @(posedge clkin) begin
    oclkreg = oclkreg + 1;
    iclkreg = iclkreg + 1;
    fork
    if (oclkreg >= divisor) begin
        oclkreg = 0;
        xmt_clock = 1;
        clko = 1;
        #1
        clko = 0;
        xmt_clock = 0;
    end
    if (iclkreg >= divisor) begin
        iclkreg = 0;
        rcv_clock = 1;
        #1
        rcv_clock = 0;
    end
    join
end
```

Figure 6.9   Clock generator

Read Operation

The read operation reads an internal register from the register file of the UART. Reading occurs on the negative edge of rd_. At that time, the model writes to the appropriate register on the bus and, on the positive edge of rd_, it tristates the bus. In addition, if the address being read is the clear-interrupt address (CLRINT_ADDR), the model resets the DONE_XMT and DONE_RCV bits of the status and clears the int output. This operation is shown in Figure 6.10.

Write Operation

Writing into a register is initiated on the negative edge of the wr_ input. The model loads the appropriate register with the value from the data bus. If the address is XMITDT_ADDR, the do_transmit event is triggered and a transmission of a byte is initiated. This operation is shown in Figure 6.11.

```
always @(negedge rd_) if (~cs_) begin
    dbus_reg = regfile[a];
    @(posedge rd_)
    dbus_reg = 8'hzz;
    if (a == CLRINT_ADDR) begin : read_block
       int = 0;
       // Reset the DONE_XMT and DONE_RCV bits in
       // the status register
       ...
    end
end
```

Figure 6.10 Read operation

```
always @(negedge wr_) if (~cs_) begin
    @(posedge wr_)
    regfile[a] = dbus;
    if (a == XMITDT_ADDR) ->do_transmit;
end
```

Figure 6.11 The write operation

Transmit Operation

Transmission is initiated by triggering the do_transmit event. First, the transmit clock is initialized, and the eight bits of the byte are transmitted serially. Second, the model sets the done bit and generates an interrupt request. This operation is shown in Figure 6.12.

Receive Operation

The receive operation is the counterpart of the transmit operation. Transmission is initiated by the UART, but reception is initiated by some external device, such as another UART.

The UART senses the start bit of a new byte when the din input goes low. When this happens, the model waits for another half clock to see if din is still low, and if so, the model starts receiving the byte. The model sets status to RECEIVING and starts sampling din at each clock.

119

```
always @do_transmit begin : transmit_block
    integer i;
    reg[7:0] data;
    reg[7:0] status;

    // Set the TRANSMITTING bit in the status register
    ...
    oclkreg = 0;
    for (i = 0; i < 8; i = i + 1) begin
      @(posedge xmt_clock)
      dout = data[i];
    end

    // Reset the TRANSMITTING bit in the status register
    // and set the DONE_XMT bit
    ...
    int = 1;
  end
```

Figure 6.12   Transmit operation

```
always @(negedge din) begin : receive_block
    integer i;
    reg[7:0] data;
    reg[7:0] status;

    // wait for half clock
    iclkreg = 0;
    while (iclkreg != divisor / 2) @clkin ;
    if (din != 0) disable receive_block;

    // Start receiving
    // Set the RECEIVING bit in the status register
    ...
    iclkreg = 0;
    for (i = 0; i < 8; i = i + 1) begin
      @(posedge rcv_clock)
      data[i] = din;
    end
    // Reset the RECEIVING bit in the status register
    // and set the DONE_RCV bit
    ...
    int = 1;
  end
```

Figure 6.13   Receive block

When done the model resets the status to DONE_RCV and raises the interrupt flag. This is shown in Figure 6.13.

Testing the Dual UART Chip

After writing the structural model of the dual UART and the functional model of the single UART, we need to develop a driver module to test the chip.

Figure 6.14 shows the top module for the chip-level simulation. It has the following parts: first, the dual UART module itself is instantiated; second, the external clock is modeled; third, some initialization takes place; fourth, some of the testing operations are coded as small tasks; fifth, the test itself is coded as an "initial" block which strings together some of the tasks into a single test; finally, a loop that observes the interrupt output from the UART and displays a message.

The following piece of code is composed of several small tasks which can be stringed together into a more complex sequence or which can be issued interactively. The first task, do_reset, issues a reset sequence by toggling the reset input. The next two tasks, writereg and readreg, initiate write and read sequences to an internal register r. They manipulate the a, cs_, wr_, and dbus inputs as required by the waveforms of Figure 6.15. The fourth task, receivebyte, initiates transmission of a byte to the UART.

The actual test consists of a reset sequence, the setting of the baud rate, a transmission of a byte, and a reception of a byte, as shown in Figure 6.16.

Implementation of the Single UART

The functional model described in the previous sections is not concerned with the efficiency, or even the feasibility, of implementation. Now, we develop a model that is more closely related to the gate-level implementation and is more amenable to synthesis.

There are two main differences between the functional model and the implementation-oriented model of the UART. One difference is that, in the latter, the register file is not implemented as an array; instead, each

121

```
module topu;
  reg [7:0] dbus_reg;
  wire [7:0] dbus = dbus_reg;
  reg[2:0] a;
  reg reset, rd_, wr_;
  reg cs_0, cs_1, din0, din1, clkin;

  wire int0, int1, dout0, dout1, clko0, clko1;

  // Instantiate the dual UART module
  dual_uart dual_uart1 (
      dbus, a, reset, rd_, wr_,
      cs_0, cs_1, din0, din1, clkin,

      int0, int1, dout0, dout1, clko0, clko1
  );


  // Generate the external clock
  parameter halfcycle = 2;
  initial clkin = 0;
  always #halfcycle clkin = ~clkin;

  initial begin
     // Set all the internal registers to 0
     ...
     #250 $finish;
  end

  // All the tasks and functions of the driver
  // are described in the following sections

  // task do_reset . . .
  // task receivebyte . . .
  // task readreg . . .
  // test_block . . .

  endmodule
```

Figure 6.14 UART test module

register is separate and is accessed by decoding the address lines a[2:0]. This enables us to set and reset single bits in the status register.

Another major difference between the two models is the replacement of the counters by shift registers. When data is transmitted or received, we need to count eight clocks, one clock per bit. In the functional model, two counters are used for this purpose. Here, we concatenate a tag to the end of the data to shift, and we detect the end of transmission when the tag has been shifted to the end of the shift register.

```
task resettask;
  begin
     reset = 1;
     #1 reset = 0;
  end
  endtask

  task writereg;
  input [2:0] r;
  input [7:0] val;
  input cs;
  begin
     a = r;
     if (cs) cs_1 = 0;
     else cs_0 = 0;
     dbus_reg = val;
     #1 wr_ = 0;
     #1 wr_ = 1;
     #1 dbus_reg = 8'hzz;
     if (cs) cs_1 = 1;
     else cs_0 = 1;
  end
  endtask

  task receivebyte;
  input [7:0] val;
  integer i;
  begin
     @(posedge clko0)
     #halfcycle
     din0 = 0;
     for (i = 0; i < 8; i = i + 1) begin
        @(posedge clko0)
        din0 = val[i];
     end
  end
  endtask

  task readreg;
  input [2:0] r;
  input cs;
  begin
     a = r;
     if (cs) cs_1 = 0;
     else cs_0 = 0;
     #1 rd_ = 0;
     #1 $display ("readreg, val = %h", dbus);
     #1 rd_ = 1;
     if (cs) cs_1 = 1;
     else cs_0 = 1;
  end
  endtask
```

Figure 6.15 Tasks of the UART test module

123

```
initial begin : test_block
    integer i;

    #1
    resettask;

    // Set the clock divider to 3
    writereg (2, 3, 0);
    writereg (3, 0, 0);

    // Start transmitting (byte 0F)
    writereg (0, 8'h0f, 0);
    wait (int0);
    #1

    // Clear the interrupt and transmit again (byte AA)
    readreg (7, 0);
    #1
    writereg (0, 8'haa, 0);
    wait (int0);
    #1

    // Clear the interrupt and receive
    readreg (7, 0);

    // Receive a byte
    receivebyte (8'hc7);
    wait (int0);
    #1
    readreg (4, 0);
    #1

    // Clear the interrupt
    readreg (7, 0);
end
always @(posedge int0) begin
    $display
  ("Received interrupt from int0,clearing at time %0d",
    $time);
end
always @(int0 or dout0 or clko0) begin
    $display
    ("int0,dout0,clko0=%b %b %b",int0,dout0,clko0);
end
```

Figure 6.16 Test block to test single_uart module

```
module uart (
    reset, dbus, a, rd_, wr_,
    cs_, din, clkin,
    int, dout, clko
);
// Input/output declarations
...

// Parameter declarations
...

reg[7:0] divmsb_reg, divlsb_reg;
reg[7:0] xmit_reg, recv_reg;
wire[15:0] divisor = { divmsb_reg, divlsb_reg };
wire[15:0] halfdivisor = { 1'b0, divisor[15:1] };
reg[15:0] oclkreg, iclkreg;
reg xmt_clock, rcv_clock;
event do_transmit;

reg transmitting;
reg receiving;
reg xmt_done;
reg rcv_done;
reg rcv_tag, xmt_tag;

wire[7:0] status =
    {4'hx,transmitting,receiving,xmt_done,rcv_done };

// Reset operation.
always @(negedge reset) begin : reset_block
    // Set all the internal registers to 0
    ...
end

// Clock generator block.
  // ...

// Read operation
function [7:0] outdbus;
input[2:0] a;
begin
    case (a)
    XMITDT_ADDR: outdbus = xmit_reg;
    STATUS_ADDR: outdbus = status;
    DIVLSB_ADDR: outdbus = divlsb_reg;
    DIVMSB_ADDR: outdbus = divmsb_reg;
    RECVDT_ADDR: outdbus = recv_reg;
    default: ;
    endcase
end
endfunction
```

continued

```
   assign int = xmt_done | rcv_done;

   always @(posedge reading) begin
      dbus_reg = outdbus (a);
      @(posedge rd_)
      dbus_reg = 8'hzz;
      if (a == CLRINT_ADDR) begin : read_block
         xmt_done = 0;
         rcv_done = 0;
      end
   end

   // Write operation.
   always @(posedge writing) begin
      @(posedge wr_)
      case (a)
      XMITDT_ADDR: begin
         xmit_reg = dbus;
         transmitting = 1;
      end
      STATUS_ADDR: { transmitting, receiving, xmt_done,
rcv_done } = dbus[3:0];
      DIVLSB_ADDR: divlsb_reg = dbus;
      DIVMSB_ADDR: divmsb_reg = dbus;
      RECVDT_ADDR: recv_reg = dbus;
      default: ;
      endcase
   end

   // Transmit operation.
   always @(posedge transmitting) begin : transmit_block
      xmt_tag = 1;
      oclkreg = 0;
   end

   always @(posedge xmt_clock) if (transmitting) begin
      // right shift the xmt_reg to dout
      { xmt_tag, xmit_reg, dout } =
         { 1'b0, xmt_tag, xmit_reg };
   end

   wire done_transmit = { xmt_tag, xmit_reg } ==
9'b000000001;

   always @(posedge done_transmit) begin
      transmitting = 0;
      xmt_done = 1;
   end

   // Receive operation.
   always @(negedge din) begin : receive_block
```

continued

```
      // wait for half clock
      ...

      // Start receiving
      receiving = 1;
      iclkreg = 0;
      { recv_reg, rcv_tag } = 9'b100000000;
   end

   wire done_receive = (rcv_tag == 1);

   always @(posedge rcv_clock)
      if (receiving)
         // right shift dout into the receive register
         { recv_reg, rcv_tag } = { din, recv_reg };

   always @(posedge done_receive) begin
      receiving = 0;
      rcv_done = 1;
   end
   endmodule
```

Figure 6.17   Implementable model for the single UART

A skeleton of the implementation-oriented model is shown in Figure
6.17.

Summary

In this chapter we demonstrated some techniques of modeling
asynchronous I/O using a UART as an example. Among the points to
note are the use of a combination of structural and behavioral models, the
handling of asynchronous bus transactions, the modeling of bidirectional
ports, the use of tasks and functions to improve readability, the use of
continuous assignments to model combinational functions, and the
construction of complex tasks from simple tasks.

The complete source code for the dual and single UART model is
given in Figure 6.18.

```
module top;
  reg [7:0] dbus_reg;
  wire [7:0] dbus = dbus_reg;
  reg[2:0] a;
  reg reset, rd_, wr_;
  reg cs_0, cs_1, din0, din1, clkin;

  wire int0, int1, dout0, dout1, clkout0, clkout1;

  // Instantiate the dual uart module
  dual_uart dual_uart1 (
     dbus, a, reset, rd_, wr_,
     130cs_0, cs_1, din0, din1, clkin,
     int0, int1, dout0, dout1, clkout0, clkout1
  );

  // Generate the external clock
  parameter halfcycle = 2;
  initial clkin = 0;
  always #halfcycle clkin = ~clkin;

  initial begin
     reset = 0;
     rd_ = 1;
     wr_ = 1;
     cs_0 = 1;
     cs_1 = 1;
     din0 = 1;
     din1 = 1;
     a = 0;
     #250 $finish;
  end

  task resettask;
  begin
     reset = 1;
     #1 reset = 0;
  end
  endtask

  task writereg;
  input [2:0] r;
  input [7:0] val;
  input cs;
  begin
     $display ("writereg, r = %0d, val = %0d, cs = %b",
            r, val, cs);
     a = r;
     if (cs) cs_1 = 0;
     else cs_0 = 0;
     dbus_reg = val;
     #1 wr_ = 0;
     #1 wr_ = 1;
     #1 dbus_reg = 8'hzz;
     if (cs) cs_1 = 1;
     else cs_0 = 1;
```

```
end
endtask

task receivebyte;
input [7:0] val;
integer i;
begin
    $display ("receivebyte, val = %0d", val);
    @(posedge clkout0)
    #halfcycle
    din0 = 0;
    for (i = 0; i < 8; i = i + 1) begin
        @(posedge clkout0)
        din0 = val[i];
        // $display ("bit = %b at time %0d", din0, $time);
    end
end
endtask

task readreg;
input [2:0] r;
input cs;
begin
    $display ("readreg, r = %0d, cs = %b", r, cs);
    a = r;
    if (cs) cs_1 = 0;
    else cs_0 = 0;
    #1 rd_ = 0;
    #1 $display ("readreg, val = %h", dbus);
    #1 rd_ = 1;
    if (cs) cs_1 = 1;
    else cs_0 = 1;
end
endtask

initial begin : test_block
    integer i;

    #1
    resettask;
    // Set the clock divider to 3
    writereg (2, 3, 0);
    writereg (3, 0, 0);
    // Start transmitting (byte 0F)
    writereg (0, 8'h0f, 0);
    wait (int0);
    #1
    // Clear the interrupt and transmit again (byte AA)
    readreg (7, 0);
    #1
    writereg (0, 8'haa, 0);
    wait (int0);
    #1
    // Clear the interrupt and receive
    readreg (7, 0);
    // Receive a byte
```

```
            receivebyte (8'hc7);
            wait (int0);
            #1
            readreg (4, 0);
            #1
            // Clear the interrupt
            readreg (7, 0);
         end

      always @ (posedge int0) begin
        $display("Received interrupt from int0, clearing at %0d",
           $time);
      end

      always @(int0 or dout0 or clkout0) begin
         $display ("int0, dout0, clkout0 = %b %b %b",
             int0, dout0, clkout0);
      end

      endmodule

/* =========================================*/
   module dual_uart (
      dbus, a, reset, rd_, wr_,
      cs_0, cs_1, din0, din1, clkin,
      int0, int1, dout0, dout1, clkout0, clkout1
   );
   inout[7:0] dbus;
   wire[7:0] dbus;
   input[2:0] a;
   wire[2:0] a;
   input reset, rd_, wr_;
   wire reset, rd_, wr_;
   input cs_0, cs_1, din0, din1, clkin;
   wire cs_0, cs_1, din0, din1, clkin;
   output int0, int1, dout0, dout1, clkout0, clkout1;
   wire int0, int1, dout0, dout1, clkout0, clkout1;

   uart u0 (
      reset, dbus, a, rd_, wr_,
      cs_0, din0, clkin,
      int0, dout0, clkout0
   );
   uart u1 (
      reset, dbus, a, rd_, wr_,
      cs_1, din1, clkin,
      int1, dout1, clkout1
   );
   endmodule

   // The functional model for the single UART
   module uart (
      reset, dbus, a, rd_, wr_,
      cs_, din, clkin,
      int, dout, clkout
   );
```

```verilog
inout[7:0] dbus;
reg [7:0] dbus_reg;
wire[7:0] dbus = dbus_reg;
input[2:0] a;
wire[2:0] a;
input reset, rd_, wr_, cs_, din, clkin;
wire reset, rd_, wr_, cs_, din, clkin;
output int, dout, clkout;
reg int, dout, clkout;

// The addresses of the internal registers
parameter
    XMITDT_ADDR = 0,
    STATUS_ADDR = 1,
    DIVLSB_ADDR = 2,
    DIVMSB_ADDR = 3,
    RECVDT_ADDR = 4,
    CLRINT_ADDR = 7;

// The internal state
parameter
    TRANSMITTING = 0,
    RECEIVING = 1,
    DONE_XMT = 2,
    DONE_RCV = 3;

reg[7:0] regfile [0:7];
wire[15:0]divisor =
    {regfile[DIVMSB_ADDR],regfile[DIVLSB_ADDR] };
reg[15:0] oclkreg, iclkreg;
reg xmt_clock, rcv_clock;
event do_transmit;

integer lines;

initial begin
    lines = 0;
    oclkreg = 0;
    iclkreg = 0;
    $monitor(
    "%m:r[0]=%h,r[1]=%h,r[2]=%h,r[3]=%h,r[4]=%h,time=%0d"
        ,regfile[0],regfile[1],regfile[2]
        ,regfile[3],regfile[4],$time);
end

/*
always @(dbus or a or reset or rd_ or wr_ or
    cs_ or din or clkin) begin
    if ((lines % 15) == 0)
        $display(
        "module dbus a reset rd_ wr_ cs_ din clkin time");
    lines = lines + 1;
    $display(
    "%m: %h    %0d    %b    %b    %b    %b    %b    %b    %0d"
        ,dbus, a, reset, rd_, wr_, cs_, din, clkin, $time);
end
```

```
*/
/*
Reset operation. On the negative edge of reset, set all the
registers to 0 and tristate the outputs.
*/
always @(negedge reset) begin : reset_block
    integer i;

    disable receive_block;
    disable transmit_block;
    oclkreg = 0;
    iclkreg = 0;
    int = 0;
    dbus_reg = 8'hzz;
    for (i = 0; i < 8; i = i + 1)
        regfile[i] = 0;
end
```

```
/*
Clock generator block. The external clock is divided by the
divisor (from regfile[3] and regfile[2]), and a divided clock
is generated for receive and transmit. The receive and
transmit clocks are of the same frequency but may be
shifted with respect to one another. The two clocks are
initialized by loading iclkreg and oclkreg.
*/
always @(posedge clkin) begin
    oclkreg = oclkreg + 1;
    iclkreg = iclkreg + 1;
    fork
    if (oclkreg >= divisor) begin
        oclkreg = 0;
        xmt_clock = 1;
        clkout = 1;
        #1
        clkout = 0;
        xmt_clock = 0;
    end
    if (iclkreg >= divisor) begin
        iclkreg = 0;
        rcv_clock = 1;
        #1
        rcv_clock = 0;
    end
    join
end
```

```
/*
Read operation. On the negative edge of rd_, put the
appropriate register on the bus, and on the positive edge of
rd_, tristate the bus. In addition, if the address being read
is the status, reset the DONE_XMT and DONE_RCV bits of the
status.
*/
always @(negedge rd_) if (~cs_) begin
    dbus_reg = regfile[a];
```

```
        @ (posedge rd_)
        dbus_reg = 8'hzz;
        if (a == CLRINT_ADDR) begin : read_block
            reg[7:0] status;
            status = regfile[STATUS_ADDR];
            int = 0;
            status[DONE_XMT] = 0;
            status[DONE_RCV] = 0;
            regfile[STATUS_ADDR] = status;
        end
    end
```

```
/*
Write operation. Load the appropriate register with the value
from the data bus. In addition, if the address indicates a
new data byte to transmit, start transmitting.
*/
    always @ (negedge wr_) if (~cs_) begin
        @ (posedge wr_)
        regfile[a] = dbus;
        if (a == XMITDT_ADDR) ->do_transmit;
    end
```

```
/*
Transmit operation. Set the status to TRANSMITTING, reset the
transmit clock, and start transmitting. When done set the
status to DONE_XMT and raise the interrupt.
*/
    always @do_transmit begin : transmit_block
        integer i;
        reg[7:0] data;
        reg[7:0] status;

    //                  $display ("In do_transmit");
        status = regfile[STATUS_ADDR];
        status[TRANSMITTING] = 1;
        regfile[STATUS_ADDR] = status;
        data = regfile[XMITDT_ADDR];
        oclkreg = 0;
        for (i = 0; i < 8; i = i + 1) begin
            @ (posedge xmt_clock)
    //                      $display ("In xmt_clock");
            dout = data[i];
        end
        status = regfile[STATUS_ADDR];
        status[TRANSMITTING] = 0;
        status[DONE_XMT] = 1;
        regfile[STATUS_ADDR] = status;
        int = 1;
    end
```

```
/*
Receive operation. On the negative edge of din, wait for
another half clock to see if din is still low, and if yes,
start receiving. Set the status to RECEIVING, and start
```

```
sampling din at each clock. When done reset the status to
DONE_RCV and raise the interrupt flag.
*/
    always @(negedge din) begin : receive_block
        integer i;
        reg[7:0] data;
        reg[7:0] status;
        /* wait_half_clock */
        iclkreg = 0;
        while (iclkreg != divisor / 2) @clkin ;
        if (din != 0) disable receive_block;
        /* Start receiving */
        status = regfile[STATUS_ADDR];
        status[RECEIVING] = 1;
        regfile[STATUS_ADDR] = status;
        iclkreg = 0;
        for (i = 0; i < 8; i = i + 1) begin
            @(posedge rcv_clock)
            data[i] = din;
        end
        regfile[RECVDT_ADDR] = data;
        status = regfile[STATUS_ADDR];
        status[RECEIVING] = 0;
        status[DONE_RCV] = 1;
        regfile[STATUS_ADDR] = status;
        int = 1;
    end

endmodule


    //      The implementation model for the single UART
    module uart (
        reset, dbus, a, rd_, wr_,
        cs_, din, clkin,
        int, dout, clkout
    );
    inout[7:0] dbus;
    reg[7:0] dbus_reg;
    wire[7:0] dbus = dbus_reg;
    input[2:0] a;
    wire[2:0] a;
    input reset, rd_, wr_, cs_, din, clkin;
    wire reset, rd_, wr_, cs_, din, clkin;
    wire reading = ~cs_ & ~rd_;
    wire writing = ~cs_ & ~wr_;

    output int, dout, clkout;
    wire int;
    reg clkout, dout;

    parameter
        XMITDT_ADDR = 0,
        STATUS_ADDR = 1,
        DIVLSB_ADDR = 2,
        DIVMSB_ADDR = 3,
```

134

```
        RECVDT_ADDR = 4,
        CLRINT_ADDR = 7;

    parameter
        TRANSMITTING = 0,
        RECEIVING = 1,
        DONE_XMT = 2,
        DONE_RCV = 3;

    reg[7:0] divmsb_reg, divlsb_reg;
    reg[7:0] xmit_reg, recv_reg;
    wire[15:0] divisor = { divmsb_reg, divlsb_reg };
    wire[15:0] halfdivisor = { 1'b0, divisor[15:1] };
    reg[15:0] oclkreg, iclkreg;
    reg xmt_clock, rcv_clock;
    event do_transmit;

    reg transmitting;
    reg receiving;
    reg xmt_done;
    reg rcv_done;
    reg rcv_tag, xmt_tag;

    wire[7:0] status =
        { 4'hx, transmitting, receiving, xmt_done, rcv_done };

/*
Reset operation. On the negative edge of reset, set all the
registers to 0 and tristate the outputs.
*/
    always @(negedge reset) begin : reset_block
        integer i;
        oclkreg = 0;
        iclkreg = 0;
        dbus_reg = 8'hzz;
        xmit_reg = 0;
        transmitting = 0;
        receiving = 0;
        xmt_done = 0;
        rcv_done = 0;
        divlsb_reg = 0;
        divmsb_reg = 0;
        recv_reg = 0;
    end

/*
Clock generator block. The external clock is divided by the
divisor (from regfile[3] and regfile[2]), and a divided clock
is generated for receive and transmit. The receive and
transmit clocks are of the same frequency but may be shifted
with respect to one another. The two clocks are initialized by
loading iclkreg and oclkreg.
*/
    always @(posedge clkin) begin
        oclkreg = oclkreg + 1;
        iclkreg = iclkreg + 1;
```

```
      fork
      if (oclkreg >= divisor) begin
         oclkreg = 0;
         xmt_clock = 1;
         clkout = 1;
         #1
         clkout = 0;
         xmt_clock = 0;
      end
      if (iclkreg >= divisor) begin
         iclkreg = 0;
         rcv_clock = 1;
         #1
         rcv_clock = 0;
      end
      join
   end
```

```
/*
Read operation. On the negative edge of rd_, put the
appropriate register on the bus, and on the positive edge of
rd_, tristate the bus. In addition, if the address being read
is the status, reset the DONE_XMT and DONE_RCV bits of the
status.
*/
```

```
   function [7:0] outdbus;
   input[2:0] a;
   begin
      case (a)
      XMITDT_ADDR: outdbus = xmit_reg;
      STATUS_ADDR: outdbus = status;
      DIVLSB_ADDR: outdbus = divlsb_reg;
      DIVMSB_ADDR: outdbus = divmsb_reg;
      RECVDT_ADDR: outdbus = recv_reg;
      default: ;
      endcase
   end
   endfunction

   assign int = xmt_done | rcv_done;

   always @(posedge reading) begin
      dbus_reg = outdbus (a);
      @(posedge rd_)
      dbus_reg = 8'hzz;
      if (a == CLRINT_ADDR) begin : read_block
         xmt_done = 0;
         rcv_done = 0;
      end
   end
```

```
/*
Write operation. Load the appropriate register with the value
from the data bus. In addition, if the address indicates a
new data byte to transmit, start transmitting.
```

136

```
*/
   always @(posedge writing) begin
      @(posedge wr_)
      case (a)
      XMITDT_ADDR: begin
         xmit_reg = dbus;
         transmitting = 1;
      end
      STATUS_ADDR:
       {transmitting,receiving,xmt_done,rcv_done}=dbus[3:0];
      DIVLSB_ADDR: divlsb_reg = dbus;
      DIVMSB_ADDR: divmsb_reg = dbus;
      RECVDT_ADDR: recv_reg = dbus;
      default: ;
      endcase
   end

/*
Transmit operation. Set the status to TRANSMITTING, reset the
transmit clock and start transmitting. When done set the
status to XMT_DONE and raise the interrupt.
*/
   always @(posedge transmitting) begin : transmit_block
      xmt_tag = 1;
      oclkreg = 0;
   end

   always @(posedge xmt_clock) if (transmitting) begin
      // right shift the xmt_reg to dout
     { xmt_tag, xmit_reg, dout } = { 1'b0, xmt_tag, xmit_reg };
   end

  wire done_transmit = { xmt_tag, xmit_reg } == 9'b000000001;

   always @(posedge done_transmit) begin
      transmitting = 0;
      xmt_done = 1;
   end

/*
Receive operation. On the negative edge of din, wait for
another half clock to see if din is still low, and if yes,
start receiving. Set the status to RECEIVING, and start
sampling din at each clock. When done reset the status to
DONE_RCV and raise the interrupt fllag.
*/
   always @(negedge din) begin : receive_block
      /* wait_half_clock */
      iclkreg = 0;
      while (iclkreg != halfdivisor) @clkin ;
      if (din != 0) disable receive_block;
      /* Start receiving */
      receiving = 1;
      iclkreg = 0;
      { recv_reg, rcv_tag } = 9'b100000000;
   end
```

```
wire done_receive = (rcv_tag == 1);

always @(posedge rcv_clock)
   if (receiving)
      // right shift dout into the receive register
      { recv_reg, rcv_tag } = { din, recv_reg };

always @(posedge done_receive) begin
   receiving = 0;
   rcv_done = 1;
end

endmodule//
```

Figure 6.18 Model for the dual and single UART

7

Modeling a Floppy Disk Subsystem

In this chapter we provide a complete example of a floppy disk subsystem (FDS) model in Verilog. Such a model may be needed when you perform a full system simulation and want to simulate the execution of code which accesses the disk. The FDS model would typically be used to perform a full functional simulation during the development of a CPU board. This example demonstrates the modeling of asynchronous systems, I/O buses, timing constraints and other techniques of writing large models.

Functional Description

Figure 7.1 shows the configuration of a typical system that includes a processor and a disk. The CPU communicates with a floppy disk controller (FDC) chip (e.g., the WD57C65) through the data and control buses. The FDC, in turn, communicates with the floppy disk drive (FDD) through two serial data lines and various control and status lines. The CPU sends commands to the FDC by writing a sequence of bytes to one of its internal registers. When the FDC receives a command, it begins to execute the command. Some commands involve reading data bytes from the CPU and sending them serially to the disk drive or reading data from the disk drive on the serial line and sending them as parallel bytes

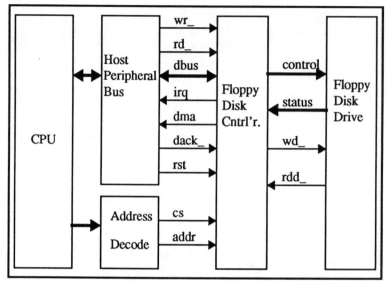

Figure 7.1 A typical CPU and floppy disk subsystem

to the CPU. The input/output pins of the controller are shown in Figure 7.2.

Since our purpose is not to design a floppy disk controller but only to develop a model in order to test the CPU design, the FDC model is greatly simplified. A real FDC chip might be able to control multiple

```
wr_          - write signal (I)
rd_          - read signal (I)
dbus         - data bus (I/O)
dma          - dma request (O)
irq          - interrupt request (O)
dack_        - dma acknowledge (I)
rst          - reset (I)
cs_          - chip select (I)
addr         - address (I)

moen_        - motor enable (O)
tr00_        - track 0 (I)
idx_         - index hole indicator (I)
rdd_         - serial data in (I)
wd_          - serial data out (O)
dirc_        - direction of head movement (O)
```

Figure 7.2 Pinout description of the controller

floppy disk drives, each drive with two heads. In this example, however, the FDC controls a single one-sided drive. Most of the signals on the CPU side are similar to those of a real FDC chip, but the signals between the FDC and the FDD have been significantly modified.

In a real controller/drive system, data is transferred on two serial lines, one for input and one for output. Because of the conflicting requirements of high data density and high reliability, the encoding techniques used to serialize and deserialize the data can be quite complex. Moreover, since the spinning speed of the drive cannot be controlled very accurately, clock information must be embedded in the data, which complicates the encoding methods even further. Recovering the clock from the data requires designing a data separator and phase-locked loop (PLL) circuit, not a trivial task.

The simplified model uses parallel 8-bit buses to transfer information between the controller and the drive and a special channel to carry the clock. This not only simplifies the coding of the model, but also speeds up the simulation while maintaining a faithful disk subsystem model with respect to the host.

Operation of the Disk Subsystem

The FDS is depicted in Figure 7.3. It has three sub modules: a timing checker, an FDC, and an FDD.

The FDC receives commands from the CPU and executes the commands. To reduce the complexity of the model, our FDC can accept only six commands, which have been greatly simplified. The FDC commands are shown in Figure 7.4.

The READ_DATA and WRITE_DATA commands read and write a single sector from the current track. The sectors on each track are ordered sequentially from 0 to SECTORS_PER_TRACK-1. FORMAT_TRACK marks the current track as formatted and writes a filler byte for all the sectors in the track. To execute a SEEK command, the FDC sets the dirc_ output and sends step pulses to the disk drive to move the disk head to the desired track. The RECALIBRATE command retracts the disk head to track 0. This is done by setting the dirc_ output and sending step pulses until the outermost track (tr00_) is active, indicating that the head is fully retracted.

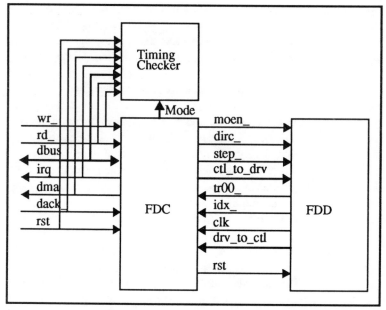

Figure 7.3 Floppy disk subsystem block diagram

Cmd #	Command name	#of bytes	Cmd code
1	READ_DATA	2	'b0110
2	WRITE_DATA	2	'b0101
3	FORMAT_TRACK	2	'b1101
4	SEEK	2	'b1111
5	RECALIBRATE	1	'b0111

Figure 7.4 Floppy disk controller commands

The following sections describe the components of the FDS model: the timing checker, the FDC and the FDD.

The Timing Checker

The timing checker is in effect not a functional part of the FDS, but it is used in modeling to detect illegal input patterns. Since these inputs are presumably generated by the CPU model, any such illegal input indicates a possible error in the design of the CPU. As it turns out, the timing checker is also useful for debugging the FDS.

The timing checker code contains two types of loops. The first type records only the time at which a signal changes its state, and the second checks for minimum or maximum delay constraints such as setup, hold, and data width times. A sample of the two types of loops is shown in Figure 7.5. The first loop in the example records the times at which the rd_ signal changes from low to high or from high to low, and the second loop checks for minimum read data width.

```
time rd_high;
wire programmed_io = (idle_mode || command_mode) && !cs_;
always @rd_ begin
        if (rd_ == 1)
                rd_high = $time;
        else if (rd_ == 0)
                rd_low = $time;
        else if (programmed_io) illegal_signal ("rd_", rd_);
end
always @ (posedge rd_) if (programmed_io)
 heckmintiming ("tRR", tRRmin, rd_low);
```

Figure 7.5 Recording and checking timing violations

The important work is done in the checkmintiming and checkmaxtiming tasks. The checkmintiming task (Figure 7.6) verifies that the time difference between two events is greater than some minimum value and the checkmaxtiming task is its counterpart for checking maximum delays. A third task, the illegal_signal task, just prints an error message and stops the simulation if an illegal signal is encountered.

The Floppy Disk Controller

The controller is divided logically into two sections: the host interface and the drive interface. The host interface section operates between the FDC and the host CPU. It accepts commands from the host and initiates their execution, sends and receives data bytes from the CPU in EXECUTE mode, and sends status information to the CPU in IDLE mode. The drive interface transfers data between the controller and the disk drive during execution, sends control signals to the drive, and receives status information from the drive.

```
task checkmintiming;
input message;
input tdiff;
input prevtime;
...
begin
 if ($time - prevtime < tdiff) begin
   $display("%m:Timing violation: %s, %0d-%0d<%0d",
       message, $time, prevtime, tdiff);
   `STOP;
 end
end
endtask
```

Figure 7.6 The checkmintiming task

The FDC has two internal registers: main_stat_reg and
main_data_reg. The main_data_reg is a general purpose 8-bit register,
which can be read and written by the processor. In COMMAND mode,
the command bytes must be written one-by-one into main_data_reg. The
main_data_reg can also be read in COMMAND mode. The
main_stat_reg is a read-only register which contains the status of the
FDC. The meaning of the various bits in the status register are given in
Figure 7.7. At the end of each command, the CPU should read the status
register and confirm the successful completion of the command.

```
parameter
  ST_COMPLETE  = 0,  // The command was completed
  ST_NOINDEX   = 1,  // Could not find the index mark
  ST_ILLEGAL   = 2,  // Illegal command
  ST_CHECKSUM  = 3,  // Bad checksum
  ST_OVERRUN   = 4,  // Overrun while sending to the host
  ST_UNDERRUN  = 5;  // Underrun while reading from the host

reg[7:0] main_stat_reg;
```

Figure 7.7 The status bits

Programmed I/O and DMA transactions

The controller can communicate with the CPU using two different
protocols: programmed I/O and direct memory access (DMA). The main
difference between the two is that programmed I/O requests are initiated

by the CPU, which uses the cs_ line to select the FDC device. Typically cs_ is decoded from a memory address or address range. DMA transfers are initiated by the FDC, and use the dma and dack_ signals for handshaking. Another difference is that in programmed I/O, the addr input selects which internal register of the FDC is read or written. In DMA mode, addr is not used.

The waveforms for programmed I/O and DMA transactions are shown in Figure 7.8, and Figure 7.9 respectively.

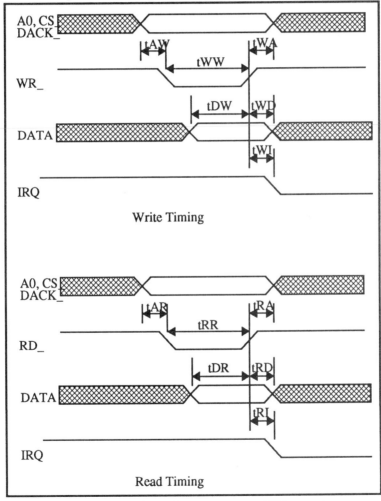

Figure 7.8 Waveforms for a programmed I/O operation

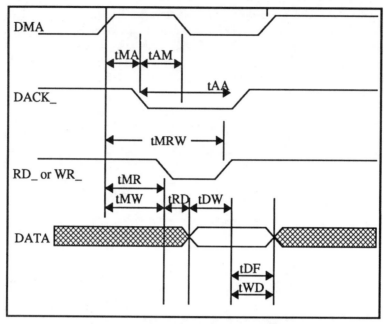

Figure 7.9 Waveforms for a DMA operation

The CPU starts a programmed I/O transaction by asserting cs_ and deasserting dack_ and setting addr. The addr input selects the desired internal register to be read or written. For a programmed read operation, the CPU asserts rd_ and reads the data off the dbus. Finally, the CPU deasserts rd_ and then deasserts cs_. The write operation is similar, except that the wr_ signal is asserted instead of the rd_, and the dbus is written by the CPU rather than read.

A DMA transaction starts when the FDC asserts the dma signal. When the CPU responds by asserting dack_, the FDC clears dma and waits for a rd_ or wr_ to be asserted. If rd_ is asserted then followed by a read operation, (i.e., the CPU reads from the FDC) and if wr_ is asserted, then a write operation is performed. The transaction ends when the rd_ or wr_ signal is deasserted, dack_ is deasserted, and the dbus is tristated. The code that initiates programmed and DMA read transactions is shown in Figure 7.10, and the code that initiates write transactions is shown in Figure 7.11.

```
always @(negedge rd_) begin
        if (dack_ == 1 && cs_ == 0) begin // Programmed read
                if (addr == MAIN_STAT)
                        dbus_reg = main_stat_reg;
                else
                        dbus_reg = main_data_reg;
                ->do_read_byte;
        end
        else if (~dack_) begin   // DMA read
                dbus_reg = byte_tofrom_host;
                #tDF dbus_reg = 8'hZZ;
        end
end
```

Figure 7.10 Programmed I/O and DMA read transactions

```
always @(posedge wr_) begin
    if (dack_ == 1 && cs_ == 0) begin // Programmed write
        if (idle_mode) begin
            current_command = 0;
            mode = `COMMAND;
        end
        main_data_reg = dbus;
        current_command = current_command + 1;
        command_array[current_command] = dbus;
        if (current_command == 1) new_command = dbus;
            if (current_command == cmd_bytes[new_command])
                begin
                mode = `EXECUTE;
                main_stat_reg = 0;
                execute;
                main_stat_reg[ST_COMPLETE] = 1;
                mode = `IDLE;
                irq = 1;
                ->unload_head;
            end
        end
    end

always @(posedge wr_) begin
    if (~dack_)      // DMA write
        byte_tofrom_host = dbus;
end
```

Figure 7.11 Programmed I/O and DMA write transactions

In IDLE mode and in COMMAND mode, the controller accepts programmed I/O requests from the CPU. In EXECUTION mode the controller initiates one DMA request for each byte to be transferred between the host CPU and the drive.

Processing the Controller Commands

The controller is always in one of three modes: IDLE, COMMAND, or EXECUTE, as shown in the code segment of Figure 7.12

After a reset or after completing the execution of a command, the FDC is in IDLE mode. In this mode the FDC waits for the host to send command bytes using programmed I/O. The first byte of a command defines the command type and implies the command length. Commands can be one or two bytes long. When the FDC receives the first byte of a new command, it switches to COMMAND mode and remains in that state until it receives the last byte of the command. When the last byte of the command is received, the FDC switches to EXECUTE mode and starts executing the command. When it finishes executing the command, the FDC switches back to IDLE mode and stays in this mode until a new command byte is transmitted by the host CPU.

The execution of the command might entail controlling the disk drive, setting parameters in the controller, or transferring data between the disk and the CPU. When the FDC completes the execution of a

```
`define IDLE     2'b00
`define COMMAND  2'b01
`define EXECUTE  2'b10

reg [1:0] mode;
wire idle_mode          = (mode == `IDLE);
wire command_mode       = (mode == `COMMAND);
wire execute_mode       = (mode == `EXECUTE);

always @(posedge rst) begin
        ...
        mode = `IDLE;
        ...
end
```

Figure 7.12 The three controller modes

command, it initiates an interrupt request by setting the irq signal, and the status of the FDC is reset to IDLE mode. The CPU can reset the interrupt request by reading the status register. A successful completion of the command is indicated by status = 8'h01.

When the controller receives a full command, it invokes the "execute" task (Figure 7.13). This task is implemented as a big case statement. It directly executes the commands SEEK and RECALIBRATE, but delegates the execution of the commands READ_DATA, WRITE_DATA, and FORMAT_TRACK to another task: read_write. The SEEK command generates step pulses until the head has

```
task execute;
begin
        case (new_command)
        READ_DATA,
        WRITE_DATA,
        FORMAT_TRACK: begin
                read_write (new_command, command_array[2]);
        end
        SEEK: begin : seek_block
                integer diff, i;
                if (current_track > command_array[2]) begin
                    diff = current_track - command_array[2];
                        dirc_ = 1;
                end
                else begin
                    diff = command_array[2] - current_track;
                        dirc_ = 0;
                end
                for (i = 0; i < diff; i = i + 1)
                        one_step;
                current_track = command_array[2];
        end
        RECALIBRATE: begin
                dirc_ = 1;
                while (tr00_)
                        one_step;
                current_track = 0;
        end
        default: begin
                main_stat_reg[ST_ILLEGAL] = 1;
                $display ("Illegal command");
                `STOP;
        end
        endcase
end
endtask
```

Figure 7.13 FDC execute task

moved to the desired track, and the RECALIBRATE command generates step pulses until the head is fully retracted and is positioned at track 0.

The read_write task is shown in Figure 7.14. It starts by loading the head and waiting for the synchronizing signal idx_. To perform the FORMAT_TRACK command, the FDC model sends bytes to the FDD, one sector at a time, until all the sectors of the track have been written. Each sector has a header (the ordinal sector number in the track), a data section (filled by some filler bytes), and a tail (a checksum of all the data

```
task read_write;
...
begin
   ->load_head;
   wait (head_is_loaded);
   main_stat_reg[ST_NOINDEX] = 1;
   @(negedge idx_)
   main_stat_reg[ST_NOINDEX] = 0;
   $display ("Detected idx_ (command %0s) at time %0t",
      cmd_names [operation], $time);
   case (operation)
   FORMAT_TRACK: begin
      for (sector = 0; sector < SECTORS_PER_TRACK;
         sector = sector + 1) begin
         ...
         // Format one sector
         ...
      end
   end
   WRITE_DATA, READ_DATA: begin
   begin : search_sector
      for (sector = 0; sector < SECTORS_PER_TRACK;
         sector = sector + 1) begin
         ...
         // If found then disable search_sector
         // Else skip this sector
         ...
      end
      $display ("Could not find the sector");
      `STOP;
      end     // search_sector block
      if (operation == WRITE_DATA)
         write_data;
      else
         read_data;
      end
   endcase
end
endtask
```

Figure 7.14 The read_write task

150

bytes and the sector head). To perform a READ_DATA or WRITE_DATA command, the FDC model searches for the appropriate sector, and then calls yet another task: write_data for writing, or read_data for reading.

The read_data and write_data tasks initiate the actual DMA transfer of bytes between the FDD and the host CPU. Each transfer has to be synchronized with the clock signal from the FDD. In order to avoid race conditions, all data is sent on the negative edge of the clock and is sampled on the positive edge of the clock. If the FDC detects a data overrun during a WRITE_DATA or READ_DATA operation, it sets the corresponding bit in the status register.

The Floppy Disk Drive

The disk drive model simulates the physical drive unit, including the actual floppy disk and the information that it contains. Figure 7.15 shows the signals which communicate between the drive and the controller.

The floppy disk itself is divided into concentric cylinders. In a multisurface disk drive, each cylinder defines concentric circles, called

```
moen_      -- Motor enable (I). When active, then after some
              delay the disk starts rotating and sends idx_
              pulses, one per rotation
dirc_      -- Direction (I). When active, then each step
              pulse moves the head one track forwards,
              otherwise, each step pulse moves the head one
              track backwards.
step_      -- Step (I). Each pulse moves the head one cylinder
              in a direction specified by dirc_.
byte_in    -- Byte_in (I). Input byte from the controller.
tr00_      -- Track zero (O). When active, it indicates that
              the head is retracted to track zero.
idx_       -- Index (O). Every revolution of the diskette,
              the drive sends a pulse to the controller. This
              indicates the beginning of the track.
clk        -- Clock (O). Used to synchronize the drive with
              thecontroller. In a real floppy drive the clock
              is derived from the data.
byte_out   -- Byte_ out (O). Output byte to the controller.
rst        -- Reset (I).
```

Figure 7.15 FDD I/O signals

tracks, one track per surface. Most floppy disk drives are double sided, i.e. they have two surfaces and two heads. Our model has only one surface, and therefor each cylinder corresponds to only one track. Tracks are further divided into sectors. Figure 7.16 depicts a floppy disk with its tracks and sectors.

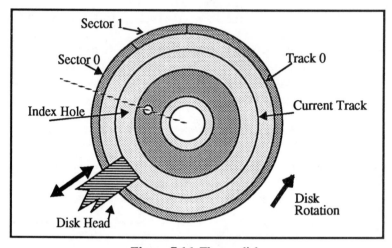

Figure 7.16 Floppy disk

The model parameterizes the size and speed of the disk (Figure 7.17). During debugging the various parameters can be modified in order to reduce the amount of data that has to be generated and checked. For example, you can create a disk with five tracks, three sectors per track, and five bytes per sector.

The disk head moves radially, and at each point in time the head is positioned above one track. This "current track" is the one that is read or written. When the head is positioned above track 0, the outermost track, the output tr00_ is active. The FDD monitors the step_ input, and each step_ pulse moves the head by one track in a direction determined by the dirc_ input. Both the FDD and the FDC models maintain their own variable representing the current track. The FDC cannot read the current track of the FDD, and the only way to synchronize the two variables is for the CPU to perform the RECALIBRATE command, which retracts the head to track 0.

```
parameter
   USECS = 10,      // Time units per microsecond
   MSECS = 10000,   // Time units per millisecond
   SECTORS_PER_TRACK = 16,
   MAX_TRACK = 96,
   DATA_PER_SECTOR = 256,
   BYTES_PER_SECTOR = DATA_PER_SECTOR + 2,
   // i.e. Data bytes + sector number + checksum
   BYTES_PER_TRACK = BYTES_PER_SECTOR * SECTORS_PER_TRACK,
   BYTES_PER_DISK = BYTES_PER_TRACK * MAX_TRACK,
   TOTAL_SECTORS = SECTORS_PER_TRACK * MAX_TRACK,
   HALF_CYCLE = 2 * USECS,
   FULL_ROTATION = BYTES_PER_TRACK * 2 * HALF_CYCLE + 200;
```

Figure 7.17 Floppy Disk Parameters

Figure 7.18 shows the model segment that implements head movement. Each negative pulse on the step_ input increments or decrements current_track, depending on the value of the direction input dirc_.

```
integer current_track;
wire tr00_ = (current_track != 0);

always @(posedge step_) begin
        if (dirc_ == 1 && current_track > 0)
                current_track = current_track - 1;
        if (dirc_ == 0 && current_track < MAX_TRACK - 1)
                current_track = current_track + 1;
end
```

Figure 7.18 Simulating disk head movement

The floppy disk has an index hole. When the disk rotates, an LED generates a pulse every time the hole passes under it. This pulse is the idx_ output from the FDD; it is used for synchronizing the FDC and the FDD. Each track is divided into SECTORS_PER_TRACK sectors which are numbered sequentially. When the FDD needs to access a sector, for example sector N, it first waits for the index signal, and then skips N-1 sectors. Figure 7.19 shows how to generate the index signal of the disk.

When the motor is on, the disk rotates and generates an index signal once per rotation. When the disk motor shuts off (moen_ == 1) and then turns back on, there is a RAMPTIME period before the signal "rotating" becomes active and enables the generation of index pulses.

153

```
reg rotating; // Indicates whether the disk is rotating

always begin
        #FULL_ROTATION
        ->do_idx;
        if (rotating) begin
                idx_ = 0;
                #1 idx_ = 1;
        end
end

always @moen_ begin
        rotating = 0;
        idx_ = 1;
        if (~moen_) begin
                #RAMPTIME
                if (~moen_) rotating = 1;
        end
end
```

Figure 7.19 Simulating disk rotation

The FDD sends data bytes to the FDC on the byte_out output and receives FDC data on the byte_in input. The transmission of bytes is synchronized by the clk signal. The clk signal is generated by the FDC and is also output to the FDC. In order to avoid race conditions, both the FDC and the FDD send the data on the negative edge of the clock and sample the data on the positive edge of the clock.

Each sector in a track is divided into a header, a body, and a tail. The header is one byte, giving the ordinal number of the sector in the track starting from 0 up to SECTORS_PER_TRACK-1. The body of the sector has DATA_PER_SECTOR data bytes, and the tail of the sector is a one-byte checksum which adds together all the bytes in the header and the body, ignoring overflow.

If the current sector is formatted, then, while the disk is rotating, the FDD continuously sends its sector data to the FDC. The FDD also continuously monitors the byte_in input. During read operation or in IDLE mode, the FDC sets the byte_in input to undefined. If this byte is not undefined (8'hxx), the byte is written on the disk as part of the header, body, or tail of the sector. Also, if any sector header is written on the track, the track is marked as formatted.

```
integer byte_index;
reg[7:0] checksum;
// one bit per track indicating
// whether the track is formatted
reg [MAX_TRACK-1:0] formatted;
reg [7:0] diskmem [0:BYTES_PER_DISK]; // Holds disk data
```

Figure 7.20 Data registers for representing the disk data

The FDD maintains several variables and arrays to represent the data on the floppy disk. These are shown in Figure 7.20.

The vector formatted has one bit per track. When this bit is on, the corresponding sector is formatted; otherwise it is unformatted. The diskmem array represents all the data on the disk, including sector heads and tail. The data is organized sequentially, one track after the other, as are the sectors within a track. The integer byte_index points to the current byte to be written and possibly read. The value of byte_index for the beginning of the current track is calculated as

```
byte_index = current_track * BYTES_PER_TRACK;
```

The byte_index variable is incremented on every negative edge of the clock each time a byte is sent to the FDC. The checksum is a global variable which keeps the checksum for the current sector. When a checksum is read from the FDC, it is compared to the internally maintained checksum, and an error is generated if they do not match.

The loop that processes the bytes of the current track is shown in Figure 7.21. First, the clock is synchronized with the index signal by disabling the clock_gen block and byte_index is initialized. Then each sector is processed: first the sector head, then its data, and finally its tail.

The processing of sector head, is very similar to the processing of sector data and sector tail. The sector_data task with the two supporting tasks sendbyte and getbyte are depicted in Figure 7.22. For each byte in the sector, the FDD first sends the byte to the FDC, on the negative edge of clk. On the positive edge of clk, it samples the data byte from the FDC. If the sampled byte is not undefined (x), then the FDD assumes that the FDC is writing, and the FDD updates the sector data. After each byte the FDD updates the checksum for the sector.

155

```
always @do_idx begin : generate_byte
        integer sector;
        disable clock_gen;
        if (~rotating) begin
                byte_out = 8'hxx;
                disable generate_byte;
        end
        byte_index = current_track * BYTES_PER_TRACK;
        for (sector = 0; sector < SECTORS_PER_TRACK;
                                    sector = sector + 1) begin
                sector_head (sector);
                sector_data;
                sector_tail;
        end
end
```

Figure 7.21 Processing a disk track

```
task sector_data;
integer i;
begin
        for (i = 0; i < DATA_PER_SECTOR; i = i + 1) begin
                @(negedge clk) sendbyte;
                @(posedge clk) if (byte_in !== 8'hxx)
                        getbyte;
                checksum = checksum + diskmem[byte_index-1];
        end
end
endtask

task sendbyte;
begin
        byte_out = diskmem[byte_index];
        byte_index = byte_index + 1;
end
endtask

task getbyte;
begin
        diskmem[byte_index - 1] = byte_in;
end
endtask
```

Figure 7.22 Processing of a sector data

Figure 7.23 shows a task that displays the disk information for debugging purposes. The sd macro is a short notation for invoking this task. This macro can be called from any Verilog naming scope because it has the full hierarchical name of the task. The macro name is kept short intentionally in order to minimize keystrokes in interactive mode.

```
`define sd test_fdc.f.di.showdisk; #0 $stop;

task showdisk;
integer i, j, k, index;
begin
    for (i = 0; i < MAX_TRACK; i = i + 1)
        begin : track_block
        if (~formatted[i]) disable track_block;
        index = i * BYTES_PER_TRACK;
        $display ("Track = %0d, index = %0d", i, index);
        for (j = 0; j < SECTORS_PER_TRACK; j = j + 1) begin
            $write ("Sector %0d: ", j);
            for (k = 0; k < BYTES_PER_SECTOR; k = k + 1) begin
                $write (" %h", diskmem[index]);
                index = index + 1;
            end
            $display (";");
        end
    end
end
endtask
```

Figure 7.23 Displaying the disk information

Testing the Subsystem

This section describes the top level test module for the FDC. The full model of test_fdc is shown with the rest of the modules at the end of this chapter. Here we shall just summarize the main points of the model. Figure 7.24 shows schematically the contents of the top module.

The global variable receiving is set to 1 during a READ_DATA command and to 0 during a WRITE_DATA command. The block that processes DMA requests checks this variable and generates an input or an output as required. The buff array has the data for one full sector of the disk.

The test_fdc module defines several utility tasks. The tasks initbuff and initbufwrite initialize buff for reading and writing respectively. The showbuf task and the sb macro are used to dump the contents of the buffer interactively. The dorst task generates a reset pulse for the controller, and the sndbyte and rcvbyte tasks send and receive one byte in programmed I/O mode. The sndcmd1 and sndcmd2 tasks send commands of length one and two respectively to the controller, and the waitdone task waits for the completion of the command.

157

```
module test_fdc;
...
// If 1 then DMA transactions read from the bus
reg receiving;
// Hold one sector worth of data
reg[7:0] buff[0:BUFFSIZE-1];
...
// Instantiate three sub modules:
// timing checker,controller and drive checktiming ct(...);
disk_controller fdc (...);
disk_drive fdd (...);

// Process DMA request by the controller
always @(posedge dma) begin
        if (receiving) begin
                // Read the data byte from the bus into buff
                ...
        end
        else begin
                // Write the data byte from buff to the bus
                ...
        end
end

// Define utility tasks
...
// Main test body
initial
        // Send command #1
        // Wait for completion
        // Send command #2
        // Wait for completion
        ...
        // Display the contents of the disk
end
endmodule
```

Figure 7.24 Test module modeling

The main body of the test sends various commands to the controller and waits for their completion. It uses the showdisk task to display the data of the disk at the end of the test.

Summary

This chapter described a complete Verilog model of a floppy disk subsystem. Although it is a simplified version of disk controller and disk drive, the model is useful for full system simulation because the intent is to debug the CPU section of the design. The final example demonstrated modeling techniques such as partitioning large models into smaller ones and using tasks, events, and functions to modularize the code and make it readable and maintainable.

The full model for the floppy disk subsystem, including the timing checker, the disk controller, the disk drive, and a top level test module, follows in Figure 7.25.

```
`define f $finish;
`define STOP $stop

module disk_controller ( rd_, wr_, cs_, dack_, addr, dbus,
    irq, dma, moen_, dirc_, step_, byte_ctl_to_drv, tr00_,
    idx_, clk, byte_drv_to_ctl, mode, rst);

input rd_;
input wr_;
input cs_;
input dack_;
input addr;
inout [7:0] dbus;
output irq;
output dma;

output moen_;
output dirc_;
output step_;
output byte_ctl_to_drv;
input tr00_;
input idx_;
input clk;
input byte_drv_to_ctl;
output[1:0] mode;
input rst;

reg irq;
reg dma;
reg[7:0] dbus_reg;
wire[7:0] dbus = dbus_reg;

reg moen_, dirc_, step_;
reg[7:0] byte_ctl_to_drv;
wire tr00_, idx_, clk;
wire[7:0] byte_drv_to_ctl;

event do_read_byte;

`define IDLE 2'b00
`define COMMAND 2'b01
`define EXECUTE 2'b10

reg [1:0] mode;
wire idle_mode = (mode == `IDLE);
wire command_mode = (mode == `COMMAND);
wire execute_mode = (mode == `EXECUTE);

/* The main status register (main_stat_reg) bits */
parameter
    ST_COMPLETE = 0, /* The command was completed */
    ST_NOINDEX = 1, /* Could not find the index mark */
    ST_ILLEGAL = 2, /* Illegal command */
    ST_CHECKSUM = 3, /* Bad checksum */
    ST_OVERRUN = 4, /* Overrun while sending to the host */
    ST_UNDERRUN = 5; /* Underrun while reading from the host */
```

```
reg[7:0] main_stat_reg;

parameter
    tDF = 1,
    tRI = 2;
parameter
    MAIN_STAT = 1,
    MAIN_DATA = 0;

reg[7:0] main_data_reg;
integer current_command; /* Index to the current command byte
                in command_array */
reg[7:0] command_array[1:2];
reg[7:0] checksum; /* The running checksum of the current
                sector */
integer current_track;

/* For debugging only*/
/*
initial begin
    $monitor ("dbus=%h, rd_=%b, wr_=%b, cs_=%b, irq=%b,
        dma=%b, dack_=%b, drv_ctl=%h, ctl_drv=%h time=%0d",
        dbus, rd_, wr_, cs_, irq, dma, dack_, byte_drv_to_ctl,
        byte_ctl_to_drv, $time); */
end
*/

parameter NCMDS = 6; /* Total number of possible commands */
integer new_command; /* The currently executing command */
parameter
    READ_DATA = 1,
    WRITE_DATA = 2,
    FORMAT_TRACK = 3,
    SEEK = 4,
    RECALIBRATE = 5,
    ILLEGAL_CMD = 0;

parameter
    USECS = 10, /* Time units per microsecond */
    MSECS = 10000, /* Time units per millisecond */
    SECTORS_PER_TRACK = 16,
    MAX_TRACK = 96,
    DATA_PER_SECTOR = 256,
    /* Data bytes + sector number + checksum */
    BYTES_PER_SECTOR = DATA_PER_SECTOR + 2,
    BYTES_PER_TRACK = BYTES_PER_SECTOR * SECTORS_PER_TRACK,
    BYTES_PER_DISK = BYTES_PER_TRACK * MAX_TRACK,
    TOTAL_SECTORS = SECTORS_PER_TRACK * MAX_TRACK,
    HALF_CYCLE = 2 * USECS,
    FULL_ROTATION = BYTES_PER_TRACK * 2 * HALF_CYCLE + 200;

integer cmd_bytes[0:NCMDS];/*command bytes for each command*/
reg [8*20:0] cmd_names [0:NCMDS];/* Command name strings */
integer cmd_code[0:NCMDS]; /* Command codes */
```

```
/*
The following three registers - SRT, HUT and HLT, hold the
delay timesfor the drive. The variable head_is_loaded
indicates whether the disk is rotating and is ready to
transfer data. The disk is shut off automatically after a
period specified in the HUT variable if there was no disk
access during this time. Once the disk is turned on, there is
a delay of HLT before it reaches full spinning speed and can
be accessed. SRT is the delay when the head is stepped from
one track to the next. The next two blocks (load_head_block
and unload_head_block) implement this automatic shutoff by
manipulating the variable "head_is_loaded" and the motor
signal "moen_".
*/

reg[3:0] SRT; /* Step Rate Time in mSecs increments */
reg[3:0] HUT; /* Head Unload Time in 16 mSecs increments */
reg[7:0] HLT; /* Head Load Time in 2 mSecs increments */
reg head_is_loaded; /* The current state of the head */
event load_head, unload_head;

always @load_head begin : load_head_block
    disable unload_head_block;
    moen_ = 0;
    #(HLT * MSECS * 2) head_is_loaded = 1;
end
always @unload_head begin : unload_head_block
    disable load_head_block;
    #(HUT * MSECS * 16) head_is_loaded = 0;
    moen_ = 1;
end

/*
The next two tasks initiate DMA transfers to and from the host
CPU respectively. They also check for overrun and underrun.
For debugging purpose, the two tasks stop when they detect
error. The real chip just set the status byte and continues.
*/

reg [7:0] byte_tofrom_host;
task send_byte_to_host;
begin
    if (dma) begin
        main_stat_reg[ST_OVERRUN] = 1;
        $display ("%m: byte overrun, byte = %h at time %0d",
            byte_tofrom_host, $time);
        `STOP;
    end
    dma = 1;
end
endtask

task get_byte_from_host;
begin
    dma = 1;
    dbus_reg = 8'hzz;
    @(negedge clk)
```

```
    if (dma) begin
        main_stat_reg[ST_UNDERRUN] = 1;
        $display ("%m: byte underrun at time %0d", $time);
        `STOP;
    end
end
endtask

/*
Move the disk head by one track. First generate a step pulse,
and then delay by the amount specified by the SRT variable
*/

task one_step;
begin
    $display ("%m: at time %0d", $time);
    step_ = 0;
    #1 step_ = 1;
    #(SRT * MSECS) ;
end
endtask

/*
The next two tasks do the DMA transfer to and from the host CPU
respectively. The data byte is transfered between the data bus
(dbus) and an internal register "byte_tofrom_host".
*/

task dmaread;
begin
    /* $display ("%m: time = %0d", $time); */
    if (~execute_mode) begin
        $display ("%m: Spurious DMA read not in execute mode");
        `STOP;
    end
    dbus_reg = byte_tofrom_host;
    #tDF dbus_reg = 8'hZZ;
end
endtask

task dmawrite;
input[7:0] byte;
begin
    /* $display ("%m: byte = %h, time = %0d", byte, $time); */
    if (~execute_mode) begin
        $display ("%m: Spurious DMA read not in execute mode");
        `STOP;
    end
    byte_tofrom_host = dbus;
end
endtask

/*
The next few blocks implement the rst rd_ and wr_ inputs from
the host CPU. These are short blocks which call other tasks
to do the actual operation.
```

```
*/

always @(posedge rst) begin
   dbus_reg = 8'hzz;
   irq = 0;
   dma = 0;
   mode = `IDLE;
   step_ = 1;
   dirc_ = 1;
   moen_ = 1;
   head_is_loaded = 0;
   disable load_head_block;
   disable unload_head_block;
end

always @(negedge rd_) begin
   if (dack_ == 1 && cs_ == 0) begin
      if (addr == MAIN_STAT)
         dbus_reg = main_stat_reg;
      else begin
         if (idle_mode)
            dbus_reg = main_data_reg;
         else begin
            $display ("Illegal read operation in mode %b",
               mode);
            `STOP;
         end
      end
      ->do_read_byte;
   end
   else if (~dack_)
      dmaread;
end

always @(posedge wr_) begin
   if (dack_ == 1 && cs_ == 0)
      programmed_write;
end

always @(posedge wr_) begin
   if (~dack_)
      dmawrite (dbus);
end

/*
The next two tasks do programmed read and write operations (as
opposed to DMA operations). They are initiated on the negative
edge of rd_ and positive edge of wr_ respectively. Depending
on the mode of the controller and on the address (addr) they
transfer the data between the internal registers and the data
bus, and possibly change the mode.
*/

task programmed_write;
begin
   if (addr != MAIN_DATA) begin
```

```
        $display ("Illegal register address: %b", addr);
        'STOP;
    end
    if (idle_mode || command_mode) begin
        if (idle_mode) begin
            current_command = 0;
            mode = 'COMMAND;
        end
        main_data_reg = dbus;
/*
The next piece of code writes one byte into the command_array
and increments the command byte counter. If a full command has
been written then go to execution mode and start executing the
command. When the command finishes executing, go back to idle
mode and generate an interrupt to the host.
*/
        current_command = current_command + 1;
        command_array[current_command] = dbus;
        if (current_command == 1) new_command = dbus;
        if (current_command == cmd_bytes[new_command]) begin
            mode = 'EXECUTE;
            main_stat_reg = 0;
            execute;
            main_stat_reg[ST_COMPLETE] = 1;
            mode = 'IDLE;
            irq = 1;
            ->unload_head;
        end
    end
    else begin
        $display ("Illegal write in unknown (%b) mode", mode);
        'STOP;
    end
end
endtask

/*
The next two blocks reset the irq and the dma outputs. The irq
is reset wheneve a byte is read, and the dma is reset whenever
the dma is acknowledged by the host processor (negative edge
of dack_).
*/

always @do_read_byte begin
    @(posedge rd_)
    fork
        #tDF dbus_reg = 8'hZZ;
        #tRI irq = 0;
    join
end
always @(negedge dack_)
    #3 dma = 0;

/*
This is the main execution task. Some of the commands (SEEK
and RECALIBRATE) execute directly. The others (READ_DATA,
```

165

```
WRITE_DATA and FORMAT_TRACK) are delegated to another task:
read_write.
*/

task execute;
begin
    $display ("%m: Executing command %0d (%0s) at time %0d",
        new_command, cmd_names[new_command], $time);
    case (new_command)
    READ_DATA,
    WRITE_DATA,
    FORMAT_TRACK: begin
        read_write (new_command, command_array[2]);
    end
    SEEK: begin : seek_block
        integer diff, i;
        if (current_track > command_array[2]) begin
            diff = current_track - command_array[2];
            dirc_ = 1;
        end
        else begin
            diff = command_array[2] - current_track;
            dirc_ = 0;
        end
        for (i = 0; i < diff; i = i + 1)
            one_step;
        current_track = command_array[2];
    end
    RECALIBRATE: begin
        dirc_ = 1;
        while (tr00_)
            one_step;
        current_track = 0;
    end
    default: begin
        main_stat_reg[ST_ILLEGAL] = 1;
        $display ("Illegal command");
        `STOP;
    end
    endcase
end
endtask

/*
This is the main task for the commands READ_DATA, WRITE_DATA
and FORMAT_TRACK. It first makes sure that the head is loaded
and then waits for the index signal synchronization. The
FORMAT_TRACK command is executed directly. For the other
commands, this task just does search for the appropriate
sector, and then delegates the actual reading and writing of
data to the tasks read_data and write_data respectively.
*/

task read_write;
input operation;
input [7:0] sec_byt;
```

166

```
integer operation;
integer sector, byte;
begin
   ->load_head;
   wait (head_is_loaded);
   $display ("%m: head is loaded at time %0d", $time);
   main_stat_reg[ST_NOINDEX] = 1;
   @(negedge idx_)
   main_stat_reg[ST_NOINDEX] = 0;
   $display ("Detected idx_ (command %0s) at time %0t",
      cmd_names [operation], $time);
   case (operation)
   FORMAT_TRACK: begin
      for (sector = 0;
         sector < SECTORS_PER_TRACK;
         sector = sector + 1) begin
         $display ("%m: Formatting sector %0d", sector);
         @(negedge clk) byte_ctl_to_drv = sector;
         checksum = sector;
         for (byte = 0;
            byte < DATA_PER_SECTOR;
            byte = byte + 1) begin
            /* $display ("Processing byte %0d", byte); */
            @(negedge clk) byte_ctl_to_drv = sec_byt;
            checksum = checksum + sec_byt;
         end
         @(negedge clk) byte_ctl_to_drv = checksum;
      end
      @(negedge clk) byte_ctl_to_drv = 8'hxx;
   end
   WRITE_DATA, READ_DATA: begin
      begin : search_sector
      for (sector = 0;
         sector < SECTORS_PER_TRACK;
         sector = sector + 1) begin
         $display ("Searching for sector = %0d", sector);
         @(posedge clk) if (byte_drv_to_ctl != sector) begin
            $display (
              "%m: Illegal sector number %0d instead of %0d",
              byte_drv_to_ctl, sector);
            'STOP;
            disable search_sector;
         end
         if (byte_drv_to_ctl == sec_byt) begin
            $display ("Found sector number (%0d)", sector);
            disable search_sector;
         end
         $disisplay(
           "%m:sector=%0d,byte_drv_to_ctl=%0d,sec_byt=%0d",
           sector, byte_drv_to_ctl, sec_byt);
         /* Still not the right sector. Skip the data */
         checksum = sector;
         for (byte = 0;
            byte < DATA_PER_SECTOR;
            byte = byte + 1) begin
            /* $display ("Processing byte %0d", byte); */
```

```
                    @(posedge clk)
                    checksum = checksum + byte_drv_to_ctl;
                end
                @(posedge clk)
                if (byte_drv_to_ctl != checksum) begin
                    main_stat_reg[ST_CHECKSUM] = 1;
                    $display ("Bad checksum");
                    `STOP;
                end
            end
            $display ("Could not find the sector");
            `STOP;
            end /* search_sector block */
            checksum = sector;
            if (operation == WRITE_DATA)
                write_data;
            else
                read_data;
        end
        endcase
end
endtask

/*
The following two tasks write and read one sector's worth of
data to or from the host CPU. The data also include the
checksum byte.
*/

task write_data;
integer byte;
begin
    $display ("%m: Write_data to sector %0d", checksum);
    for (byte = 0;
         byte < DATA_PER_SECTOR;
         byte = byte + 1) begin
        get_byte_from_host;
        checksum = checksum + byte_tofrom_host;
        byte_ctl_to_drv = byte_tofrom_host;
    end
    get_byte_from_host;
    if (checksum != byte_tofrom_host) begin
        $display ("%m: Bad chacksum, %h, should be %h",
         byte_tofrom_host, checksum);
        `STOP;
    end
    byte_ctl_to_drv = byte_tofrom_host;
    @(negedge clk)
    byte_ctl_to_drv = 8'hxx;
end
endtask

task read_data;
integer byte;
begin
    $display ("Read_data from sector %0d", checksum);
```

```
        byte_tofrom_host = checksum;
        send_byte_to_host;
        for (byte = 0;
             byte < DATA_PER_SECTOR;
             byte = byte + 1) begin
           @(posedge clk)
           checksum = checksum + byte_drv_to_ctl;
           byte_tofrom_host = byte_drv_to_ctl;
           /*$display("%m:Sending byte %0d(=%h) at host at %0d",
            byte, byte_drv_to_ctl, $time); */
           send_byte_to_host;
        end
        @(posedge clk)
        byte_tofrom_host = checksum;
        $display ("%m: Sending checksum byte %h to host at %0d",
           byte_drv_to_ctl, $time);
        send_byte_to_host;
        @(negedge dma) ;
        @(posedge rd_) ;
end
endtask

/* Initialize the various command arrays */
initial begin : set_arrays
   integer i;
   cmd_bytes[READ_DATA] = 2;
   cmd_bytes[WRITE_DATA] = 2;
   cmd_bytes[FORMAT_TRACK] = 2;
   cmd_bytes[SEEK] = 2;
   cmd_bytes[RECALIBRATE] = 1;
   cmd_bytes[ILLEGAL_CMD] = 0;

   cmd_names[READ_DATA] = "READ_DATA";
   cmd_names[WRITE_DATA] = "WRITE_DATA";
   cmd_names[FORMAT_TRACK] = "FORMAT_TRACK";
   cmd_names[SEEK] = "SEEK";
   cmd_names[RECALIBRATE] = "RECALIBRATE";
   cmd_names[ILLEGAL_CMD] = "ILLEGAL_CMD";

   for (i = 0; i <= NCMDS; i = i + 1)
      cmd_code[i] = ILLEGAL_CMD;
   cmd_code['b00110] = READ_DATA;
   cmd_code['b00101] = WRITE_DATA;
   cmd_code['b01101] = FORMAT_TRACK;
   cmd_code['b01111] = SEEK;
   cmd_code['b00111] = RECALIBRATE;
   SRT = 2;
   HUT = 3;
   HLT = 5;
end
endmodule /* disk_controller */


/* ======================================================= */
```

```
This is the top module that is used to test the fdc module.
It has one instance of fdc and behavioral code to generate
test vectors on the inputs of the fdc and to observe the output
of the fdc.
*/

module test_fdc;
reg [7:0] dbus_reg;
wire [7:0] dbus = dbus_reg;
reg rst, rd_, wr_, cs_, dack_;
reg addr;
reg debug;
reg receiving;

parameter BUFFSIZE = 1024;
reg [7:0] buff[0:BUFFSIZE-1]; /* Hold one sector worth of data
*/
integer nbuff; /* The number of data in the buffer */

parameter
    MAIN_STAT = 1,
    MAIN_DATA = 2;
parameter
    READ_DATA = 1,
    WRITE_DATA = 2,
    FORMAT_TRACK = 3,
    SEEK = 4,
    RECALIBRATE = 5,
    ILLEGAL_CMD = 0;


/* Wires connecting the controller to the drive */
wire moen_, dirc_, step_, tr00_, idx_, clk;
wire [7:0] byte_ctl_to_drv, byte_drv_to_ctl;

wire [1:0] mode;

/* Check input signal validity */
checktiming ct (rd_, wr_, cs_, dack_, addr, dbus, mode);

/* Do CPU interface */
disk_controller fdc (rd_, wr_, cs_, dack_, addr, dbus, irq,
dma,
    moen_, dirc_, step_, byte_ctl_to_drv, tr00_, idx_,
    clk, byte_drv_to_ctl, mode, rst);

/* Do floppy drive interface */
disk_drive fdd (moen_, dirc_, step_, byte_ctl_to_drv, rst,
    tr00_, idx_, clk, byte_drv_to_ctl);

/* Process DMA request by the controller */
always @(posedge dma) begin
    if (receiving) begin
        #1 dack_ = 0;
        #2 rd_ = 0;
        #1 buff[nbuff] = dbus;
```

```
            nbuff = nbuff + 1;
            #3 rd_ = 1;
            #1 dack_ = 1;
        end
        else begin
            /* $display ("%m: sending buff[%0d] = %h", nbuff,
buff[nbuff]); */
            #1 dack_ = 0;
            dbus_reg = buff[nbuff];
            #2 wr_ = 0;
            nbuff = nbuff + 1;
            #3 wr_ = 1;
            #1 dbus_reg = 8'hzz;
            dack_ = 1;
        end
end

/* Initialize the buffer for reading from the controller */
task initbuff;
integer i;
begin
    for (i = 0; i < BUFFSIZE; i = i + 1)
        buff[i] = 8'hxx;
    nbuff = 0;
end
endtask

/* Initialize the buffer for writing to the controller */
task initbuffwrite;
integer i;
begin
    for (i = 0; i < BUFFSIZE; i = i + 1)
        buff[i] = i;
    nbuff = 0;
end
endtask

/* A task and a macro to show the contents of the buffer */
`define sb showbuff; #0 $stop; .
task showbuff;
integer i, j, linesize;
reg nonx;
begin
    for (i = 0; i < BUFFSIZE; i = i + linesize) begin
        nonx = 0;
        linesize = 20;
        if (i + linesize > BUFFSIZE) linesize = BUFFSIZE - i;
        for (j = i; j < i + linesize; j = j + 1)
            if (buff[j] !== 8'hxx) nonx = 1;
        if (nonx) begin
            $write ("\nbuff[%d]: ", i);
            for (j = i; j < i + linesize; j = j + 1)
                $write (" %h", buff[j]);
        end
    end
    $display ("");
```

```
end
endtask

/* Reset the controller */
task dorst;
begin
    rst = 1;
    #100 rst = 0;
end
endtask

/*
The next two tasks send and receive one byte from the
controller in programmed mode.
*/

task sndbyte;
input [7:0] byte;
input add;
begin
    if (debug)
        $display ("%m: byte = %h, add = %b, time = %0d",
         byte, add, $time);
    cs_ = 0;
    addr = add;
    #2 wr_ = 0;
    #1 dbus_reg = byte;
    #10 wr_ = 1;
    #2 cs_ = 1;
    dbus_reg = 8'hzz;
end
endtask

task rcvbyte;
output [7:0] byte;
input add;
begin
    $display ("%m: address = %b", add);
    cs_ = 0;
    addr = add;
    #2 rd_ = 0;
    #1 byte = dbus;
    #3 rd_ = 1;
    #1 cs_ = 1;
    $display ("Received byte = %h", byte);
end
endtask

/*
The next two tasks send commands of length 1 and 2
respectively to the controller. They call the task sndbyte
with address MAIN_DATA.
*/
```

```
task sndcmd1;
input[7:0] cmd;
begin
    $display ("%m: cmd = %h", cmd);
    if (irq) begin
        $display ("%m: irq is high, cannot initiate a
command");
        $stop;
    end
    sndbyte (cmd, MAIN_DATA);
end
endtask

task sndcmd2;
input [7:0] cmd;
input [7:0] byte1;
begin
    $display ("%m: cmd = %h, byte1 = %h",
        cmd, byte1);
    if (irq) begin
        $display ("%m: irq is high, cannot initiate a
command");
        $stop;
    end
    sndbyte (cmd, MAIN_DATA);
    sndbyte (byte1, MAIN_DATA);
end
endtask

task waitdone;
reg [7:0] status;
begin
    wait (irq);
    #1
    rcvbyte (status, MAIN_STAT);
    if (status != 1) begin
        $display ("%m: Status = %b (instead of 00000001 at time
%0d", status, $time);
        $stop;
    end
    wait (~irq);
end
endtask

/*
The actual test is composed of a string of lower level tasks.
The following actions take place:
1. Reset the controller.
2. Send the RECALIBRATE command to retract head to track 0.
3. Send a SEEK comand to move the head to track 3.
4. Send two FORMAT commands for the current track
   (one of the commands is redundant).
5. Send a READ_DATA command to read the formatted track
   sector.
6. Send a WRITE_DATA command to write on one of the sectors.
*/
```

```
initial begin
$monitor ("irq = %b at time %0d", irq, $time);
    debug = 0;
    rst = 0;
    rd_ = 1;
    wr_ = 1;
    cs_ = 1;
    dack_ = 1;
    #1 dorst;
    sndcmd1 (RECALIBRATE);
    waitdone;
    sndcmd2 (SEEK, 3);
    waitdone;
    sndcmd2 (FORMAT_TRACK, 8'h33);
    waitdone;
    initbuff;
    receiving = 1;
    sndcmd2 (READ_DATA, 1);
    waitdone;
    showbuff;
    receiving = 0;
    initbuffwrite;
    sndcmd2 (WRITE_DATA, 0);
    waitdone;
    $display ("Test complete");
    showbuff;
    test_fdc.fdd.showdisk;
    $stop;
end

endmodule /* test_fdc */


/* ======================================================== */
module checktiming (rd_, wr_, cs_, dack_, addr, dbus, mode);
input rd_;
input wr_;
input cs_;
input dack_;
input addr;
input[7:0] dbus;
input[1:0] mode;
wire execute_mode = (mode == 'EXECUTE);
wire idle_mode = (mode == 'IDLE);
wire command_mode = (mode == 'COMMAND);

/*
The following parameters are the various timing constraints as
specified in the data sheet and shown in the waveform diagram.
For simplification, all the delays are assumed to be 0 or 1
time units. The actual delays are given in the comments, in
nanoseconds. The variables that follow remember the time at
which the various signals have changed. These times are used
when the timing constraints are checked.
*/
```

```
parameter
   tARmin = 1, /* 10 */
   tRRmin = 1, /* 80 */
   tRAmin = 0,
   tAWmin = 1, /* 10 */
   tWDmin = 1, /* 70 */
   tWAmin = 0;
time rd_high,rd_low,wr_high,cs_low,dack_high,addrchanged;

wire programmed_io = (idle_mode || command_mode) && !cs_;

/*
The folloing three short tasks are used for improved
readability. The first task just prints a message and stops.
The second task checks for minimum delay violation and stops
if one is detected, and the third one checks for maximum delay
violation. The tasks call the macro `STOP which is defined as
$stop, however, the macro can be modified to be null, so that
timing violations are reported but simulation continues.
*/

task illegal_signal;
input signame;
input sigval;
reg [8*20:0] signame;
reg sigval;
begin
    $display ("%m: Illegal signal %s = %b at time %0d",
        signame, sigval, $time);
    `STOP;
end
endtask

task checkmintiming;
input message;
input tdiff;
input prevtime;
reg [8*20:0] message;
integer tdiff;
time prevtime;
begin
    if ($time - prevtime < tdiff) begin
        $display ("%m: !! Timing violation: %s, %0d - %0d <
%0d",
            message, $time, prevtime, tdiff);
        `STOP;
    end
end
endtask

task checkmaxtiming;
input message;
input tdiff;
input prevtime;
reg [8*20:0] message;
```

```
integer tdiff;
time prevtime;
begin
    if ($time - prevtime > tdiff) begin
        $display ("%m: Timing violation: %s, %0d - %0d > %0d",
            message, $time, prevtime, tdiff);
        `STOP;
    end
end
endtask

initial begin
    rd_high = 0;
    rd_low = 0;
    wr_high = 0;
    cs_low = 0;
    dack_high = 0;
    addrchanged = 0;
end

/*
The following few blocks just record the time at which the
various bus signal have been modified. These times are later
used to do timing checks.
*/

always @rd_
    if (rd_ == 1)
        rd_high = $time;
    else if (rd_ == 0)
        rd_low = $time;
    else if (programmed_io) illegal_signal ("rd_", rd_);

always @wr_
    if (wr_ == 1)
        wr_high = $time;
    else if (programmed_io && wr_ != 0)
        illegal_signal ("wr_", wr_);

always @cs_
    if (cs_ == 0)
        cs_low = $time;
    else if (cs_ != 1)
        illegal_signal ("cs_", cs_);

always @dack_
    if (dack_ == 1)
        dack_high = $time;

always @addr addrchanged = $time;

/*
The rest of the blocks do the actual timing checks by calling
the previously defiined tasks.
*/
```

```
always @(negedge rd_) if (programmed_io) begin
   checkmintiming ("tAR to cs_", tARmin, cs_low);
   checkmintiming ("tAR to addr", tARmin, addrchanged);
   checkmintiming ("tAR to dack_", tARmin, dack_high);
end

always @(negedge wr_) if (programmed_io) begin
   checkmintiming ("tAW to cs_", tAWmin, cs_low);
   checkmintiming ("tAW to addr", tAWmin, addrchanged);
   checkmintiming ("tAW to dack_", tAWmin, dack_high);
end

always @(posedge rd_) if (programmed_io) begin
   checkmintiming ("tRR", tRRmin, rd_low);
end

always @dbus if (programmed_io) begin
   checkmintiming ("tWD", tWDmin, wr_high);
end

always @(posedge cs_ or negedge dack_ or addr) begin
   checkmintiming ("tRAmin", tRAmin, rd_high);
   checkmintiming ("tWAmin", tWAmin, wr_high);
end
endmodule


/* ================================================== */
/*
The disk drive model simulates the physical drive unit,
including the actual floppy disk and the information that it
contains. The following signals communicate between the drive
and the controller:

moen_    -- Motor enable (low active). Input. When active, then
         after some delay the disk starts rotating and sending
         idx_ pulses.
dirc_    -- Direction (low active). Input. When active, then each
         step pulse moves the head outside, otherwise, each step
         pulse moves the head back inside.
step_    -- Step (low active). Input. Each pulse moves the head
         one
         cylinder in a direction specified by dirc_.
byte_in  -- Byte input. Input. Input byte from the controller.
tr00_    -- Track zero (low active). Output. When active, it
         indicates that the head is retracted to track zero.
idx_     -- Index (low active). Output. Every revolution of the
         diskette, the drive sends a pulse to the controller.
         This indicates the beginning of the track
         (first sector).
clk      -- Clock. Output. Used to synchronize the drive with the
         controller. In a real floppy drive the clock is derived
         from the data.
byte_out -- Byte output. Output. Output byte to the
         controller.
rst      -- Reset
```

177

```
*/

module disk_drive (moen_, dirc_, step_, byte_in, rst,
    tr00_, idx_, clk, byte_out);

input moen_;
input dirc_;
input step_;
input [7:0] byte_in;
input rst;

output tr00_;
output idx_;
output clk;
output [7:0] byte_out;

parameter
    USECS = 10, /* Time units per microsecond */
    MSECS = 10000, /* Time units per millisecond */
    SECTORS_PER_TRACK = 16,
    MAX_TRACK = 96,
    DATA_PER_SECTOR = 256,
    BYTES_PER_SECTOR = DATA_PER_SECTOR + 2, /* Data bytes +
sector number + checksum */
    BYTES_PER_TRACK = BYTES_PER_SECTOR * SECTORS_PER_TRACK,
    BYTES_PER_DISK = BYTES_PER_TRACK * MAX_TRACK,
    TOTAL_SECTORS = SECTORS_PER_TRACK * MAX_TRACK,
    HALF_CYCLE = 2 * USECS,
    FULL_ROTATION = BYTES_PER_TRACK * 2 * HALF_CYCLE + 200;

parameter RAMPTIME = 10 * MSECS; /* uSecs for full speed */

event do_idx;
integer byte_index;
reg [7:0] checksum;
reg idx_;
reg clk;
reg [7:0] byte_out;
reg [MAX_TRACK-1:0] formatted;/*One bit per track indicating
                /* whether the track s formatted or not */
reg rotating; /* Indicates whether the disk is rotating */
reg [7:0] diskmem [0:BYTES_PER_DISK]; /* Holds the disk data*/
integer current_track;
wire tr00_ = (current_track != 0);

task init;
integer i;
begin
    $display ("The total number of bytes is %0d",
BYTES_PER_DISK);
    $display ("Full rotation = %0d uSecs", FULL_ROTATION);
    for (i = 0; i < MAX_TRACK; i = i + 1)
        formatted[i] = 0;
    idx_ = 1;
    current_track = 0;
    rotating = 0;
```

```
end
endtask

initial init;

/*
The following block implements the head movement. The variable
current_track is the current track. Each (negative)
pulse on the step_ input increments or decrements
current_track,
depending on the value of the direction input (dirc_).
*/

always @(posedge step_) begin
    if (dirc_ == 1 && current_track > 0)
        current_track = current_track - 1;
    if (dirc_ == 0 && current_track < MAX_TRACK - 1)
        current_track = current_track + 1;
end

/*
The following two blocks generate the index signal of the
disk. Whenever the motor is on, the disk rotates and generates
an index signal once per rotation. Whenever the disk motor
shuts off (moen_ == 1) and then turns on, there is a RAMPTIME
period before the signal "rotating" turns on.
*/

always begin
    #FULL_ROTATION
    ->do_idx;
    if (rotating) begin
        idx_ = 0;
        #1 idx_ = 1;
    end
end

always @moen_ begin
    rotating = 0;
    idx_ = 1;
    if (~moen_) begin
        #RAMPTIME
        if (~moen_) rotating = 1;
    end
end

/*
The next two blocks implement the clock generation. The clock
starts operating when the disk rotates. It is also
synchronized to the index signal every full rotation.
*/

always @(negedge rotating) disable clock_gen;

always begin : clock_gen
integer cycle;
```

```
      wait (rotating);
      cycle = 0;
      forever begin
         clk = 1;
         #HALF_CYCLE clk = 0;
         #HALF_CYCLE clk = 1;
         cycle = cycle + 1;
      end
end

/*

While the disk is rotating, the following generate_byte block
checks if the track is formatted. If so, then generate_byte
generates clocks and data, one per byte. It does it in three
sections, sector head, sector data and sector tail. Sector
head just sends
*/

always @do_idx begin : generate_byte
   integer sector;
   disable clock_gen;
   if (~rotating) begin
      byte_out = 8'hxx;
      disable generate_byte;
   end
   byte_index = current_track * BYTES_PER_TRACK;
   for (sector = 0; sector < SECTORS_PER_TRACK;
               sector = sector + 1) begin
      sector_head (sector);
      sector_data;
      sector_tail;
   end
end

always @(posedge rst) begin
   $display ("%m: reset");
   disable generate_byte;
   disable clock_gen;
   disable sector_head;
   disable sector_data;
   disable sector_tail;
end

always @(negedge rotating) disable generate_byte;

/*
The next few short tasks are used for transferring data bytes
between the disk drive and the controller. The bytes in the
drive are organized in one big array. A global variable
byte_index holds the index to the next byte in the array which
should be read or written, and this index is incremented after
every transfer.
*/
```

```
task sendbyte;
begin
    /* $display ("%m: byte_index = %0d", byte_index); */
    byte_out = diskmem[byte_index];
    byte_index = byte_index + 1;
end
endtask

task sendbyte_x;
begin
    /* $display ("%m: byte_index = %0d", byte_index); */
    byte_out = 8'hxx;
    byte_index = byte_index + 1;
end
endtask

task getbyte;
begin
    /* $display ("%m: byte_index-1 = %0d, byte_in = %h",
        byte_index-1, byte_in); */
    diskmem[byte_index - 1] = byte_in;
end
endtask

/*
The following three tasks do the actual transfer of the sector
head, sector data and sector tail respectively. The sector
head is one byte containing the ordinal number of the sector
on the track (starting from zero). The sector data contains
DATA_PER_SECTOR contiguous bytes, and the sector tail is a one
byte checksum, which is calculated as the sum of all the data
bytes and the sector number, ignoring overflow. The disk drive
communicates with the controller by two 8 bit buses, one
transfers bytes from the drive to the controller and the other
transfers bytes from the controller to the drive. Data are
presented on these buses on the negative edge of the clock
(clk) and are sampled
on the positive edge of the clock. The drive always sends the
sector information on the outgoing bus. It updates the disk
data only if the incoming byte is not 8'hxx.
*/

task sector_head; input sector; integer sector; begin
    /* $display ("%m: sector = %0d", sector); */
    checksum = diskmem[byte_index];
    @(negedge clk)
    if (formatted[current_track]) sendbyte;
    else sendbyte_x;
    @(posedge clk) if (byte_in !== 8'hxx) begin
        getbyte;
        formatted[current_track] = 1;
    end
end
endtask

task sector_data;
integer i;
```

```
begin
    for (i = 0; i < DATA_PER_SECTOR; i = i + 1) begin
        @(negedge clk) sendbyte;
        @(posedge clk) if (byte_in !== 8'hxx)
            getbyte;
        checksum = checksum + diskmem[byte_index-1];
    end
end
endtask

task sector_tail;
begin
    /* $display ("%m"); */
    @(negedge clk) sendbyte;
    @(posedge clk) if (byte_in !== 8'hxx)
        getbyte;
    if (checksum != diskmem[byte_index - 1]) begin
        $display ("%m: Bad checksum %h, should be %h",
            diskmem[byte_index-1], checksum);
        $stop;
        diskmem[byte_index-1] = checksum;
    end
end
endtask

/*
The following task displays the disk information for debugging
purposes. The macro sd is a short notation for invoking this
task. This macro can be called from any $scope, since it has
the full hierarchical name of the task
*/

`define sd test_fdc.f.di.showdisk; #0 $stop; .
task showdisk;
integer i, j, k, index;
begin
    for (i = 0; i < MAX_TRACK; i = i + 1) begin : track_block
        if (~formatted[i]) disable track_block;
        index = i * BYTES_PER_TRACK;
        $display ("Track = %0d, index = %0d", i, index);
        for (j = 0; j < SECTORS_PER_TRACK; j = j + 1) begin
            $write ("Sector %0d: ", j);
            for (k = 0; k < BYTES_PER_SECTOR; k = k + 1) begin
                $write (" %h", diskmem[index]);
                index = index + 1;
            end
            $display (";");
        end
    end

end
endtask

endmodule /* disk_drive */
```

Figure 7.25 Complete model for the Floppy Disk Controller

8

Useful Modeling and Debugging Techniques

Learning to design and simulate in Verilog is more than just learning the syntax and semantics of the language. As in every learning process, the best way to learn is by doing. As you start using the language, you will develop your own style of design, and you will discover techniques for modeling in Verilog. In this chapter we present some useful tips and techniques that we hope will help you in developing your own techniques on the way to mastering Verilog.

Bidirectional Ports

A bidirectional port operates as either an input or an output, depending on a control variable. Typically, a data bus is shared among the CPU, the memory system, and other peripheral devices and operates as a bidirectional port. At any time, only one device can write to the bus and the rest of the devices can only read.

A port in Verilog can be designated as input, output or inout. In a Verilog behavioral model, the input ports are wires and the output ports are registers. A bidirectional (inout) port can be specified as a wire which accepts its value from a "shadow register" through a continuous assignment. When the port is enabled as an output, you set the value of the shadow register to the desired output value. When the port is disabled for output and should operate as an input, simply set the shadow register to Z. This enables other signal input to the port.

Figure 8.1 shows a complete example of modeling a bidirectional port. Figure 8.2 shows a block diagram of a CPU with memory. The data bus is bidirectional, and depending on whether the CPU reads from memory or writes to memory, the data port operates as an input or an output. The signal waveforms are shown in Figure 8.3 and Figure 8.4. When the memory senses the read signal, it puts the appropriate data on the data bus; the data port is an output from the memory and is an input to the CPU. When the memory senses a negative transition on the write signal, it stores the value from the data bus to the appropriate address; the data port is an output from the CPU and is an input to the memory.

```
module top;
wire [31:0] address;
wire [15:0] data;
wire read, write;

   cpu u1 (data, address, read, write);
   mem u2 (data, address, read, write);

endmodule

module cpu (data, address, read, write);
output [31:0] address;
inout  [15:0] data;
output read, write;

reg  [31:0] address;
reg  [15:0] data_reg;
wire [15:0] data = data_reg;
reg  read, write;

reg  [15:0] somedata;

   initial
      data_reg = 16'hzzzz;

task writetomem;
input [31:0] taddress;
input [15:0] tdata;

begin
   data_reg = tdata;
   #1 write = 1;
   #20 write = 0;                              continued
```

```
  #1 data_reg = 16'hzzzz;
end

endtask

task readfrommem;
input   [31:0] taddress;
output [15:0] tdata;

begin
   read = 1;
   #20 tdata = data;
   #1 read = 0;
end

endtask

   initial begin
      ......
      writetomem (32'h100, 16'h5555);
      ......
      readfrommem (32'h104, somedata);
      ......
   end
   ...
endmodule

module mem (data, address, read, write);
input [31:0] address;
inout [15:0] data;
input read, write;

wire [31:0] address;
reg   [15:0] data_reg;
wire [15:0] data = data_reg;
wire read, write;

reg   [15:0] memarr [0:1023];

always @(posedge write) begin
   @(negedge write)
   memarr[address] = data;
end

always @(posedge read) begin
   data_reg = memarr[address];
   @(negedge read)
   data_reg = 32'hzzzzzzzz;
end

endmodule
```

Figure 8.1 Code for modeling a bidirectional port

185

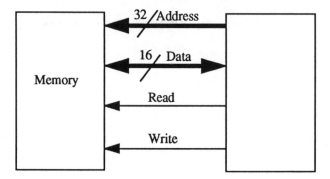

Figure 8.2 CPU block diagram

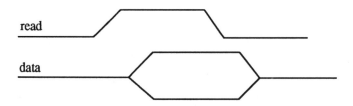

Figure 8.3 Waveform timing diagram for a read cycle

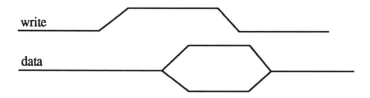

Figure 8.4 Waveform timing diagram for a write cycle

Bus Transactions in a Pipeline Architecture

It is common in a pipeline architecture for bus transactions to expand over multiple cycles. Usually such transactions are interleaved to maintain the throughput of one transaction per cycle. Consider a CPU/ memory system, in which the address is transferred to the address bus in two cycles. The address bus has four fields as follows:

33	32	17	16	15	0
W	M5B[15:0]		V	LSB[15:0]	

When bit 33, the W bit, is 1, the current transaction is a write transaction; otherwise it is a read transaction. Bits 32-17 are the 16 most significant address bits of the current transaction. Bit 16, the V bit, if 1, indicates that the previous transaction was valid; otherwise abort the previous transaction. Bits 15-0 are the least significant bits of the previous transaction. Figure 8.5 depicts a snapshot of the address bus where the number in brackets indicates the transaction number.

```
W[1]   MSB[1]     V[0]   LSB[0]
W[2]   MSB[2]     V[1]   LSB[1]
W[3]   MSB[3]     V[2]   LSB[2]
W[4]   MSB[4]     V[3]   LSB[3]
W[5]   MSB[5]     V[4]   LSB[4]
W[6]   MSB[6]     V[5]   LSB[5]
```

Figure 8.5 Address bus transactions

It is desirable to write a task that accepts as input the four fields of an address bus transaction (W, MSB, V, and LSB) and generates the transaction. Such encapsulation enables you to issue transactions from different locations in the code. More importantly, you can issue transactions interactively from the terminal. A straightforward approach of modeling such a task is depicted in Figure 8.6. Note that addressbus[33:0] was declared previously in the module. c

But the task as written above is not sufficient. If two consecutive bus transactions are needed, the following statements will not work:

```
@clock #1 addrtrans ('x100, 1, 1);
@clock #1 addrtrans ('x102, 1, 0);
```

Since each execution of the task takes two clock cycles, the second call to the addrtrans task occurs two clock cycles after the first one. In other words, there is no way to execute two transactions on two consecutive clock cycles; thus the effect of the pipeline can not be simulated. One way to try to correct this problem is to use events as shown in Figure 8.7.

```
task addrtrans;
input [31:0] address;
input valid;
input write;

begin
    @clock
    addressbus[33:17] = { write, address[31:16] };
    @clock
    addressbus[16:0] = { valid, address[15:0] };
end

endtask
```

Figure 8.6 Modeling bus transactions

```
......
reg   [15:0] msb_address, lsb_address;
reg   vld, wrt;
event do_trans;

task addrtrans;
input [31:0] address;
input valid;
input write;

begin
    msb_address = address[31:16];
    lsb_address = address[15:0];
    vld = valid;
    wrt = write;
    ->do_trans;
end

endtask

    always @do_trans begin : trans_block
        @clock
        addressbus[33:17] = { wrt, msb_address };
        @clock
        addressbus[16:0] = { vld, lsb_address };
    end
```

Figure 8.7 An attempt to solve the multiple-cycle transactions

This solution has an advantage over the Figure 8.6 model in that the addrtran task takes no simulation time to execute. In effect, the task does not perform the transaction, but just triggers it. The actual transaction is being done by trans_block. However, each loop takes two cycles to execute, so that the code in Figure 8.7 still does not work. The first transaction starts execution, and one clock into the transaction the do_trans event is triggered again; but this event is lost because the *always* loop did not complete and is not waiting for the event to be triggered.

To solve this problem, we use two always loops and two events. As before, the task just triggers an event that enables an always loop. This time, however, the loop is only one clock long, and triggers another event that enables the second always loop (Figure 8.8).

```
......
reg    [15:0] msb_address, lsb_address, lsb_address1;
reg    vld, wrt, vld1;
event do_trans_cycle1, do_trans_cycle2;

task addrtrans;
input [31:0] address;
input valid;
input write;

begin
   msb_address = address[31:16];
   lsb_address = address[15:0];
   vld = valid;
   wrt = write;
   ->do_trans_cycle1;
end

endtask

   always @do_trans_cycle1 begin
      @clock
      addressbus[33:17] = { wrt, msb_address };
      vld1 = vld;
      lsb_address1 = lsb_address;
      ->do_trans_cycle2;
   end

   always @do_trans_cycle2 begin
      @clock
      addressbus[16:0] = { vld1, lsb_address1 };
   end
```

Figure 8.8 A correct way to model multiple bus transactions

The extension to longer transactions of three or more cycles is straightforward. Use a sequence of always loops, each of them lasting one cycle and triggering an event that enables the next cycle. Notice that you also need temporary global variables that pass the pipeline values from cycle to cycle. In the example above these variables are msb_address, lsb_address, lsb_address1, vld, wrt, and vld1.

Combinational Blocks with Unknown Inputs

The outputs of a combinational block might have known values even when the inputs are unknown. The simplest example of such a case is an AND gate that has one input X and another input 0. In such a case, Verilog recognizes that the output of the gate must be 0. A slightly more complicated example is a 2-to-1 selector in which both inputs are 0 and the select input is X (Figure 8.9). Even though the output is 0 no matter what the select input is, Verilog does not recognize it and instead propagates an X to the output. One way to get the correct result is to

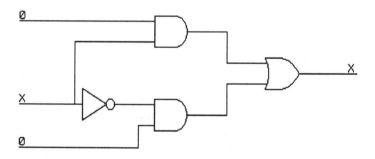

Figure 8.9 Unknown inputs in combinational networks

design a selector UDP that exhibits the desired behavior under all input conditions. This might not be feasible for more complicated circuits.

In Verilog, an X value on a signal can have two different causes. One cause is that two different sources try to drive the same net (using the same strength) to two different logical values. This is usually a design error. The other possible cause for an X is that a signal has not been initialized. Sometimes an uninitialized signal also indicates a design error; but X's during the first cycles of initialization are legitimate, and a designer can exploit the cases where the output is independent of the X inputs in order to optimize the design.

Suppose that a state machine is described in Espresso (UC Berkeley) format, and that some entries in the state table have remained unspecified to optimize design. In order to force the output to a known value, you may have to force all the inputs to some arbitrary (but known) values. You can insert a buffer device that converts X to 1 (or 0) as shown in Figure 8.10. The implementation of such a device is given in Figure 8.11.

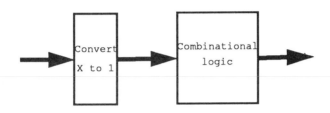

Figure 8.10 Converting unknown inputs to known inputs

```
module xto0 (out, in);
output out;
input  in;

   wire out = (in == 1) ? 1 : 0;

endmodule
```

Figure 8.11 A device for converting unknown signals

Large Memory as a Table Lookup

When modeling a large memory subsystem, you might encounter degradation in simulation performance. Verilog itself does not place any limit on the size of memory array, but if the memory has an address space of four gigabytes, chances are that the operating system will not be able to allocate space for such a large array. One way to solve the problem is

191

to use a table lookup technique (or associative memory) to simulate the physical memory.

Our first solution assumes that memory access is highly localized; namely, that at each point in time only a small fraction of the memory is used. For example, let's assume that only sixteen memory locations are used at any one time. Two arrays are provided: one for memory addresses and one for memory contents. Whenever we access a memory location, all memory addresses are scanned to see if a named address is in use. If the address is in use, the corresponding memory contents array location is used for reading or writing. If this memory location is not being used, the address and contents are inserted into the two arrays. In the latter case, another memory location may have to be replaced, using, say, least-recently-used (LRU) algorithm.

If we attempt to read a nonexisting memory location, the program prints an error message and stops. Figure 8.12 shows the code for the memory module. For simplicity, this model does not use the LRU algorithm to release array locations; instead, a rotating counter selects the next location to be released.

The solution in Figure 8.12 is effective only for very localized memory access. If our program uses a large memory in a random way, this scheme can be very slow. Every time memory is accessed, the complete array (16 here) is scanned for the required address. If the array size must be increased to say, 4096, simulation may run too slowly. Here we can borrow an algorithm from software engineering, called "hash table access," to reduce search time.

Assume that we will access no more than 4096 memory locations, scattered randomly between 0 and 1 megabytes. In this solution, as in the previous one, we have two arrays: one for addresses and one for contents. Instead of scanning all the addresses, a hash function converts the real address into an index to the tables. The arrays' size is 5041 (a prime number about 1.2 times larger than the total number of entries), and the hash function is the remainder of the real address when divided by the hash table size. Figure 8.13 shows the hash function for accessing a memory location. Figure 8.14 and Figure 8.15 show the tasks for accessing and modifying memory locations using the hashing technique.

The readdata function handles hash collisions in the search_address block. When two addresses hash to the same location, a

192

simple (though not necessarily efficient) method of resolving the conflict: a linear scan of the table to find a free location. If none is available, the hash table is full and a message is printed. The model stops at this point.

Loading Interleaved Memory

Normally, when modeling a memory subsystem, the contents of memory reside in a disk object file and is loaded into a Verilog memory array during initialization. The compiler generates the object code

```
module memory (address, data, rd, wr);
input [31:0] address;
inout [15:0] data;
input rd, wr;

parameter MEMSIZE = 16;

wire [31:0] address;
reg  [15:0] data_reg;
wire [15:0] data = data_reg;
wire rd, wr;

reg [31:0] address_array[0:MEMSIZE-1];
reg [15:0] data_array[0:MEMSIZE-1];

integer lastwritten;

    initial
        lastwritten = 0;

    always @(posedge wr) begin : write_cycle
        integer i;
        #1 // Set up time
        /*
        First see if this address exists in the address_array
         if yes, then just replace the data in this
         address; otherwise
         replace the data in the location specified by
         lastwritten.
        */
        for (i = 0; i <= 15; i = i + 1)
           if (address_array[i] == address)
              lastwritten = i;
        address_array[lastwritten] = address;
        data_array[lastwritten] = data;
        lastwritten = (lastwritten + 1) % 16;
    end // write_cycle
```

continued

```
always @(posedge rd) begin : read_cycle
     integer i;
     integer found;
     found = 0;
     /*
     See if the address exists in the address_array. If
     yes, then fetch the data; otherwise print an
     error message and stop the simulation. Wait for
     the negative edge of read and tristate the data bus.
     */
     for (i = 0; i <= 15; i = i + 1)
        if (address_array[i] == address) begin
           found = 1;
           data_reg = data_array[i];
        end
     if (found == 0) begin
        $display (
        "Trying to read nonexisting data fromaddress %h",
             address);
        $stop;
     end
     @(negedge rd)
     data_reg = 16'hzzzz;
  end // read_cycle

endmodule
```

Figure 8.12 Associative array for simulating large memory

```
. . . . .
`define HASHSIZE 5041
reg  [31:0] address_tab [0:`HASHSIZE-1];
reg  [31:0] data_tab [0:`HASHSIZE-1];

initial begin : intitialize_hashtab
   integer i;
   for (i = 0; i < `HASHSIZE; i = i + 1)
      address_tab[i] = 'hxxxxxxxx;
   end
end

function integer hash;
input [31:0] address;

   hash = address % `HASHSIZE;

endfunction
```

Figure 8.13 Hash function and hash table initialization

```
function [31:0] readdata;
input [31:0] address;
integer index, i;

begin
   index = hash (address);
   if (address_tab[index] == address)
      readdata = data_tab[index];
   else begin : search_address
      // The first hashing did not produce the right address
      // Start scanning the table for the address
      for (i = (index + 1) % `HASHSIZE;
           i != index;
           i = (i + 1) % `HASHSIZE) begin
           // Due to hash collisions,address was installed
           if (address_tab[index] == address) begin
              readdata = data_tab[index];
              disable search_address;
           end
           else if (address_tab[index] === 'hxxxxxxxx) begin
              $display (
    "%m: Trying to read uninitialized data at address %h",
              address);
              $stop;
              disable search_address;
           end
      end
      $display ("%m: Hash table is full");
      $stop;
   end
end

endfunction
```

Figure 8.14 Accessing a memory location using the hash method

assuming a single sequential and contiguous memory. In that case, it can be loaded into internal arrays using Verilog's $readmemb or $readmemh task. However, simulating interleaved memory requires some special steps.

Let us consider a two-way interleaved memory. The concept is easily extended to multiway interleaving. A 256-word memory, mem, can be implemented by two 128-word memories, mem1 and mem2, where mem1 holds even addresses (0,2,4,...126) and mem2 holds odd addresses (1,3,5,...127). The size of each word is identical in mem, mem1, and mem2. This is called "horizontal interleaving".

```
task writedata;
input [31:0] address;
input [31:0] value;
integer index, i;

begin
   index = hash (address);
   if (address_tab[index] == address)
     data_tab[index] = value;
   else begin : search_address
     // The first hashing did not produce the right address
     // Start scanning the table for the address
     for (i = (index + 1) % `HASHSIZE;
          i != index;
          i = (i + 1) % `HASHSIZE) begin
        if (address_tab[index] == address) begin
           //Due to hash collisions, address was installed
            disable search_address;
        end
        else if (address_tab[index] === 'hXXXXXXXX) begin
           data_tab[index] = value;
           address_tab[index] = address;
           disable search_address;
        end
     end
     // The whole table was searched for an empty slot
     $display ("%m: Hash table is full");
     $stop;
   end
end

endtask
```

Figure 8.15 Modifying a memory location using the hash method

The model shown in Figure 8.16 takes the object code from a file prog.file and loads it into mem1 and mem2 with even and odd addresses respectively. The memaccess task reads and writes data to or from the appropriate memory bank, given an address and the type of the operation (read or write). The least significant address bit, address[0], is decoded to determine in which memory bank the address will be found. This procedure is equivalent to asserting a chip select signal for one of the two memory banks from the least significant bit and using the rest of the high order bits, address[ASIZE-1:1], to access the appropriate location.

The memaccess task does not have to be as trivial as shown here. A complete handshake protocol for memory access can be implemented as a part of this task. Nevertheless, no matter how complex the task

```
module interleaved_memory;
parameter       DSIZE = 32,
                ASIZE = 8,
                MAXWORDS = 1 << ASIZE,   // = 256
                HALFMAX = MAXWORDS/2 ;

reg [DSIZE-1:0] MEM[0:MAXWORDS-1],
                MEM1[0:HALFMAX-1],
                MEM2[0:HALFMAX-1] ;

integer i, j;

task memaccess (address, data, rw) ;
input [ASIZE-1:0] address ;
inout [DSIZE-1:0] data ;
input rw ;
reg   [ASIZE-2:0] addr ;

begin
   addr = address[ASIZE-1:1] ;
   if (address[0] == 0) begin : even_address
      if (rw == 1) // even_read
         data = MEM1[addr] ;
      else          // even_write
        MEM1[addr] = data ;
   end
   else begin : odd_address
      if (rw == 1) // odd_read
         data = MEM2[addr] ;
      else          // odd_write
        MEM2[addr] = data ;
   end
end

endtask

   initial begin : loadmem
      j = 0 ;
      $readmemh("PROG.FILE",MEM) ;
      for (i=0; i < MAXWORDS; i=i+2) begin
         MEM1[j] = MEM[i] ;
         MEM2[j] = MEM[i+1] ;
         j = j + 1 ;
      end
   end
endmodule
```

Figure 8.16 A model for loading interleaved memory

becomes, it provides a transparent interface between the memory implementation and the rest of the system.

The description shown in Figure 8.16 is inefficient. This becomes evident when the memory size is very large. Notice that we declared three memories—mem, mem1, and mem2. The total number of memory words used during the simulation is

```
maxwords+halfmax+halfmax = 2*maxwords
```

or twice the size of a single contiguous memory. A large memory leads to swapping- and paging-related problems because the simulator needs to allocate physical (or virtual) memory to hold the contents of these simulated memories. Unfortunately, in Verilog simulator, there is no way to "release" a memory. This implies that although mem was used only for the purpose of loading the contents of the object code from the file into interleaved memory banks, it occupies runtime memory of the simulator but remains unused.

To work around the simulator problem, one approach is to write a simple C program that generates two files, prog.file1 and prog.file2, by writing out alternate lines of object code from prog.file. Now the declaration for mem can be deleted and the $readmemh statement can be replaced by the following:

```
$readmemh("PROG.FILE1", MEM1) ;
$readmemh("PROG.FILE2", MEM2) ;
```

The example shown in Figure 8.17 accomplishes the same task in Verilog instead of in C. In either approach it is a two-step process: first convert a single object code file into two object code files, and then read these object code files into the appropriate memory banks at the start of the simulation. This approach eliminates the use of mem completely, using only the required simulated and physical memories.

Verification of Setup and Hold Constraints

In many design projects, you have to write not only the module being designed but also the external environment around the module. For example, when designing a microprocessor chip, you may have to design a model for the memory subsystem, the disk subsystem, the keyboard, or the console. The purpose of this environment is to generate stimuli for the module being designed and to collect and display simulation results.

```
module splitfiles ;
parameter DSIZE = 32 ,
          ASIZE = 8,
          MAXWORDS = 1 << ASIZE ;
integer i, f1, f2 ;

   reg [DSIZE-1:0] MEM[MAXWORDS-1:0] ;

   initial begin
      $fopen("PROG.FILE1",f1) ;
      $fopen("PROG.FILE2",f2) ;
      $readmemh("PROG.FILE",MEM) ;
      for (i=0; i<MAXWORDS; i = i+2) begin
         $fdisplayh(f1,MEM[i] ;
         $fdisplayh(f2,MEM[i+1] ;
      end
end
endmodule
```

Figure 8.17 An efficient model for loading interleaved memory

Many times the environment models must check the timing relationships among signals on the I/O ports of the module being designed. For example, if the module is a Micro Channel bus controller, then it has to obey some setup and hold constraints. Such checks can be isolated in separate processes (always loops) which continuously monitor the signals in question and their relationships. Chapter 7 shows the use of such checks where the floppy disk controller, acting as part of the simulation environment, checks the correctness of the signals produced by the host CPU interface.

Effects of Verilog Execution Order and Scheduling

A Verilog model has to be analyzed in the context of the Verilog scheduling algorithm. The real hardware operates in real parallelism; however, simulating the hardware on a machine with a single CPU implies that two events cannot occur simultaneously, even if they occur at the same simulated time. This phenomenon can be sometimes confusing, and the following two examples demonstrate its effect. Consider the Verilog model in Figure 8.18.

Although the expression a & b is continuously assigned to wire c, the assignment does not take effect immediately when a or b changes. Instead, the Verilog simulator just schedules an event that recomputes the value of c whenever a or b changes, and continues to execute the next

```
module m;
   reg a, b;
   wire c = a & b;
   initial begin
      a = 1;
      b = 1;
      //#0 ;  Enable this statement to see c modified
      $display ("a = %b, b = %b, c = %b", a, b, c);
   end
endmodule
```

Figure 8.18 Effect of Verilog event scheduling

statements until it encounters a timing control construct (@, #, or wait). At that time the simulator executes the event to compute the value of c.

In order to see the effect of the continuous assignment, simply insert a zero delay statement (#0 ;) just before the $display statement. This reschedules the $display statement to the end of the current simulation time, by which time the effect of changing a and b has propagated to c.

Figure 8.19 illustrates another example of the same phenomenon. Here we trigger an event that is supposed to modify a variable. Triggering the event just schedules the execution of the task but does not yet execute the task. Here too, inserting a zero delay statement immediately before the $display statement executes the e_block.

Another common situation where event scheduling can be misleading is where a module has both behavioral and structural instances. Suppose that you have a combinational block which you want to test for speed. One way to do this is to write a top module that instantiates one copy of the module under test, and to have a behavioral instance that generates the input test patterns as shown in Figure 8.20.

If you run the module as shown in Figure 8.20 you will discover that it executes very quickly, and that the $display statement is executed only once at the end of the simulation. The loop that assigns the input to the combinational module executes as a single event, so the combinational block never gets control to execute its function until the loop

```
module m;
integer a, b, c;
event    e;

   always @e begin : e_block
      c = a + b;
   end

   initial begin
      a = 1;
      b = 2;
      ->e;
      // #0 ;// Enable this statement to see c modified
      $display ("a = %d, b = %d, c = %d", a, b, c);
   end

endmodule
```

Figure 8.19 Effect of Verilog event scheduling

terminates and relinquishes control to the event scheduler. By modifying the statement

```
        inreg = i;
```

to

```
        #0 inreg = i;
```

you can remedy the problem and the test will execute as intended.

```
module comb (in1, in2, in3, in4, in5, out1, out2);
input  in1, in2, in3, in4, in5;
output out1, out2;
        assign { out1, out2 } = in1+in2+in3+in4+in5;
endmodule

module top;
reg  [4:0] inreg;
wire [1:0] outwire;
integer    i;

parameter testsize = 5000;

   comb c (inreg[4], inreg[3], inreg[2], inreg[1], inreg[0],
           outwire[1], outwire[0]);
   initial
      for (i = 0; i < testsize; i = i + 1)
         inreg = i;
   always @outwire
      $display ("outwire = %b", outwire);

endmodule
```

Figure 8.20 Test for combinational module execution speed

Generation of Test Vectors for Complex Modules

The best way to obtain test data is from a real system. For example, in a model of a computer system, you can load the memory with a test program and begin executing the program on the model. Sometimes, you may get a trace file from running the actual device in a test environment while collecting the data (e.g., with a logic analyzer). More often than not, you must write your own test program. It is usually advantageous to develop the tests from the bottom up, writing small tasks to perform trivial operations and stringing them into more complicated tasks.

We exemplify this technique by developing a test for a memory subsystem module. The most basic operations on the memory are read from an address and write to an address. Figure 8.21 shows the code to implement the two tasks. It assumes the control signals cs_ (chip select), rd_ (read), and wr_ (write).

```
task readmem;
input   [MEMSIZE:0] addr;
output [DATSIZE:0] val;
begin
   abus = addr;
   #1 cs_ = 0;
   #1 rd_ = 0;
   #1 val = dbus;
   rd_ = 1;
   cs_ = 1;
   #1 ;
end
endtask

task writemem;
input   [MEMSIZE:0] addr;
input [DATSIZE:0] val;
begin
   abus = addr;
   cs_ = 0;
   dbusreg = val;
   #1 wr_ = 0;
   #1 wr_ = 1;
   #1 cs_ = 1;
   dbusreg = 8'hzz;
end
endtask
```

Figure 8.21 Basic test tasks for memory testing

```
task initmem;
input start, finish, pattern;
integer start, finish, pattern;
begin : initmem_block
integer i;
    for (i = start; i <= finish; i = i + 1)
        writemem (i, pattern+i);
end
endtask

task copymem;
input source, dest, size;
integer source, dest, size;
begin : copymem_block
integer i;
reg[DATSIZE:0] tmp;
    for (i = 0; i <= size; i = i + 1) begin
        readmem (source + i, tmp);
        writemem (dest + i, tmp);
    end
end
endtask

task comparemem;
input source, dest, size;
integer source, dest, size;
begin : comparemem_block
integer i;
reg[DATSIZE:0] tmp1, tmp2;
    for (i = 0; i <= size; i = i + 1) begin
        readmem (source + i, tmp1);
        readmem (dest + i, tmp2);
        if (tmp1 != tmp2) begin
                $display
                ("%m: error,mem[%h](%h)!=mem[%h](%h)",
                source+i, tmp1, dest+i, tmp2);
            $stop;
        end
    end
end
endtask
```

Figure 8.22 Second-level test tasks for memory testing

Having written the basic tasks, we can easily write more
complicated tasks that are based on them. For our purpose we need three
compound tasks: one for initializing the memory, one for copying a block
from one location in memory to another, and one for comparing two
blocks of memory. All of these tasks are shown in Figure 8.22.

Finally we use the second-level tasks to build even a higher level task. This task can perform a complete test by initializing the memory, copying a block of memory to a different address, and comparing the source with the destination (Figure 8.23).

A skeleton for the full module is given in Figure 8.24. Increasing the nesting depth of task calls could affect the efficiency of simulation. However, it is usually preferable to defer efficiency considerations to a later stage of simulation, when speed becomes more important. It is much easier to take a readable model and improve its efficiency than to start with a poorly written model and make it more readable and maintainable.

```
task test;
input start, finish, pattern;
integer start, finish, pattern;
begin : test_block
integer size, middle;
    size = (finish - start) / 2;
    middle = start + size;
    initmem (start, finish, pattern);
    copymem (start, middle, size);
    comparemem (start, middle, size);
end
endtask
```

Figure 8.23 Driver for memory testing

Verification of the Test Vectors

In many cases, test vector generation is only part of the test generation problem. Analyzing test results and verifying their correctness is also a major task. If you have a way to generate the expected results, you can use Verilog or some utility to automatically compare the expected results with the actual ones. If you do not have an easy way to generate the expected results, then, by judiciously selecting the test vectors, you can simplify the process of inspecting and verifying the simulation results. Of course, test vector generation is case-specific; but we can demonstrate the technique by using an example.

```
module test_mem;
parameter
   MEMSIZE = 10,
   DATSIZE = 8,
   MAXADDR = (1 << MEMSIZE) - 1;
wire [DATSIZE-1:0] dbus;
reg [MEMSIZE-1:0] abus;
reg [DATSIZE-1:0] dbusreg;
reg cs_, wr_, rd_;

mem m (rd_, wr_, cs_, abus, dbus);

task readmem;
...
endtask

task writemem;
...
endtask

...

initial begin
   test (0, 100, 0);
   test ('hff, 'hfff, 'haa);
   ...
end

endmodule
```

Figure 8.24 Skeleton of the full test module

Consider a barrel shifter that is a part of an ALU:

```
module shifter (
        in32,    // 32 bit input
        cin,     // carry in
        shft,    // 5 bit shift amount
        byte,    // byte operation (8 bit)
        word,    // word operation (16 bit)
        double,  // double word operation (32 bit)
        dir,     // direction (0 - left, 1 - right)
        op,      // 2 bit operation:
                        // 00 - shift logical
                        // 01 - shift arithmetic
                        // 10 - rotate
                        // 11 - rotate with cary
        out32,   // 32 bit output
        cout     // carry out
);
```

Clearly the size of the input prohibits exhaustive testing. Using random tests makes it excruciatingly difficult to confirm the correctness of the results. Instead we will design the test based on the expected result.

The shifter has four operations which have to be tested in two directions, with two different carry bit values, and with three different input widths (byte, word, and double word mode)—a total of 4*2*2*3 = 48 sections. A typical output section for, say, left shift arithmetic with carry set and byte mode looks like the example shown in Figure 8.25. The pattern in the figure is regular and can be easily verified by visual inspection.

The other sections of the test can be designed in a similar way, and the printout can be set in a way that shows at a glance that the output is correct.

```
in32 = 00000000000000000000000010000000
  cin = 1, b = 1, w = 0, d = 0
  dir = 1 (left), op = 01 (shift arithmetic)

shift   cout                    out32
----    ----                    -----
  0      1      00000000000000000000000010000000
  1      1      00000000000000000000000011000000
  2      1      00000000000000000000000011100000
  3      1      00000000000000000000000011110000
  4      1      00000000000000000000000011111000
  5      1      00000000000000000000000011111100
  6      1      00000000000000000000000011111110
  7      1      00000000000000000000000011111111
  8      1      00000000000000000000000011111111
```

Figure 8.25 Test vectors organized for ease of inspection

Summary

This chapter presented a collection of techniques that can useful when writing Verilog models. As you gain experience, you will be able to develop your own techniques. But, while writing more and more complex models, don't forget that the most important quality of good Verilog code is its readability. Use meaningful variable names, modularize your code into tasks and functions, use indentation to show the block structure, and use comments to explain the functionality of your code.

A P P E N D I X

Verilog Formal Syntax Definition

This appendix describes the Verilog HDL syntax. The syntax is given in extended BNF notation. The following conventions are used: items within sharp brackets (<>) are nonterminals. Keywords are given in bold characters. A star (*) indicates that the previous construct can appear zero or more times. A question mark (?) indicates that the previous item is optional, i.e. it can appear zero or one time. One common construct in Verilog is a list of items separated by commas:

```
item, item, .... , item
```

which in BNF can be described as

```
<list_of_items> := <item> <,<item>>*
```

In order to reduce the size of the BNF description, we will omit the definitions of such lists.

```
<verilog_file>
   := <module>*

<module>
   := module <module_name> <module_ports>? ;
      <module_items>*
      endmodule

<module_ports>
   := (<list_of_ports>?)

<module_name>
   := <IDENTIFIER>

<port>
   := <port_expression>?
   |  . <port_name> ( <port_expression>? )

<port_expression>
   := <port_reference>
   |  { <port_reference> <, <port_reference>>* }

<port_reference>
   := <variable_name>
   |  <variable_name> [ <expression> ]
   |  <variable_name> [ <expression> : <expression> ]

<port_name>
   := <IDENTIFIER>

<variable_name>
   := <IDENTIFIER>

<module_item>
   := <parameter_declaration>
   |  <input_declaration>
   |  <output_declaration>
   |  <inout_declaration>
   |  <net_declaration>
   |  <reg_declaration>
   |  <integer_declaration>
   |  <gate_instantiation>
   |  <module_instantiation>
   |  <udp_instantiation>
   |  <always_instantiation>
   |  <initial_instantiation>
   |  <continuous_assignment>
   |  <function>
```

```
<function>
   := function <range>? <function_name> ;
      <func_declaration>*
      <statement_or_null>
      endfunction

<function_name>
   := <IDENTIFIER>

<func_declaration>
   := <parameter_declaration>
    | <input_declaration>
    | <reg_declaration>
    | <integer_declaration>

<parameter_declaration>
   := parameter <range>? <list_of_assignments> ;

<input_declaration>
   := input <range>? <list_of_variables> ;

<output_declaration>
   := output <range>? <list_of_variables> ;

<inout_declaration>
   := inout <range>? <list_of_variables> ;

<net_declaration>
   := <NETTYPE> <charge_strength>? <expandrange>? <delay>?
      <list_of_variables> ;

    | <NETTYPE> <drive_strength>? <expandrange>? <delay>?
      <list_of_assignments> ;

<NETTYPE>
   := wire

<expandrange>
   := <range>

<reg_declaration>
   := reg <range>? <list_of_register_variables> ;

<integer_declaration>
   := integer <list_of_integer_variables> ;

<continuous_assignment>
   := assign <drive_strength>? <delay>?
       <list_of-assignments> ;
```

```
<initial_instantiation>
    := initial statement
    |  initial <seq_block>

<always_instantiation>
    := always <statement>
    |  always <seq_block>

<variable_name>
    := <IDENTIFIER>

<register_variables>
    := <IDENTIFIER>

<integer_variable>
    := <IDENTIFIER>

<range>
    := [ <expression> : <expression> ]

<gate_instantiation>
    := <GATETYPE> <drive_strength>? <delay>?
       <gate_instance> <, <gate_instance>>* ;

<GATETYE>
    := and
    |  nand
    |  or
    |  nor
    |  xor
    |  xnor
    |  buf
    |  not

<gate_instance>
    := <gate_instance_name>? ( <terminal> <,terminal>>* )

<gate_instance_name>
    := <IDENTIFIER>

<terminal>
    := <identifier>
    |  <expression>

<module_instantiation>
    := <module_name> <module_instance> <,<module_instance>>*;

<module_name>
    := <IDENTIFIER>
```

```
<module_instance>
    := <module_instance_name> ( <list_of_module_terminals>? )

<module_instance_name>
    := <IDENTIFIER>

<module_terminal>
    := <identifier>
    |  <expression>

<named_port_connection>
    := . IDENTIFIER ( <identifier> )
    |  . IDENTIFIER ( <expression> )

<statement>
    := <assignment>
    |  if ( <expression> ) <statement_or_null>
    |  if ( <expression> ) <statement_or_null>
       else <statement_or_null>
    |  case ( <expression> ) <case_items>+
       endcase
    |  for ( <assignment> ; <expression> ; <assignment> )
           <statement>
    |  <seq_block>
    |  disable <IDENTIFIER> ;

<assignment>
    := <lvalue> = <expression>

<case_item>
    := <expression> <,<expression>>* : <statement_or_null>
    |  default : <statement_or_null>
    |  default <statement>

<seq_block>
    := begin
           <statement>*
       end
    |  begin : <block_name>
           <block_declaration>*
           <statement>*
       end

<block_name>
    := <IDENTIFIER>
```

```
<block_declaration>
    := <parameter_declaration>
    |  <reg_declaration>
    |  <integer_declaration>

<lvalue>
    := <IDENTIFIER>
    |  <IDENTIFIER> [ <expression> ]
    |  <concatenation>

<expression>
    := <primary>
    |  <UNARY_OPERATOR> <primary>
    |  <expression> <BINARY_OPERATOR> <expression>
    |  <expression> ? <expression> : <expression>

<UNARY_OPERATOR> is one of the following tokens:
    + - ! ~ & ~& | ^| ^ ~^

<BINARY_OPERATOR> is one of the following tokens:
    + - * / % == != === !== && || < <= > >= & | ^ ^~ << >>

<primary>
    := <number>
    |  <identifier> [ <expression> ]
    |  <identifier> [ <expression> : <expression> ]
    |  <concatenation>
    |  <multiple_concatenation>
    |  <function_call>
    |  ( <expression> )

<number>
    := <NUMBER>
    |  <BASE> <NUMBER>
    |  <SIZE> <BASE> <NUMBER>

<NUMBER> is any number made of the following characters:
    0123456789abcdefABCDEF

<BASE> is one of the following tokens:
    'b 'B 'o 'O 'd 'D 'h 'H

<SIZE> is any number of following digits: 0123456789

<concatenation>
    := { <expression> <,<expression>>* }

<multiple_concatenation>
    := { <expression> <,<expression>>* } }
```

```
<function_call>
    := <function_name> ( <expression> <,<expression>>* )

<function_name>
    := <IDENTIFIER>

<delay>
    := # <NUMBER>
    |  # <identifier>
    |  ( <expression> <, <expression>>* )
```

<IDENTIFIER>

An identifier is any sequence of letters, digits, and the underscore '_' symbol, except that the first character must be a letter or underscore. Upper and lower case letters are considered to be different. Identifiers may be of any size and all characters are significant.

A P P E N D I X

B

Verilog Keywords

This appendix describes the reserved words of Verilog hardware description language.

and	always	assign	begin
buf	bufif0	bufif1	case
cmos	deassign	default	defparam
disable	else	end	endcase
endfunction	endmodule	endprimitive	endtable
endtask	event	for	force
forever	fork	function	highz0
highz1	if	initial	inout
input	integer	join	large
medium	module	nand	negedge
nor	not	notif0	notif1
nmos	or	output	parameter
pmos	posedge	primitive	pulldown
pullup	pull0	pull1	rcmos
reg	release	repeat	rnmos
rpmos	rtran	rtranif0	rtranif1
scalared	small	specify	specparam
strong0	strong1	supply0	supply1
table	task	tran	tranif0
tranif1	time	tri	triand
trior	trireg	tri0	tri1
vectored	wait	wand	weak0
weak1	while	wire	wor
xnor	xor		

ORDER FORM

Automata Publishing Company
10487 Westacres Dr. Cupertino CA 95014
Phone: 408-255-0705   Fax: 415-855-9545

Name: _____

Title: _____

Company: _____

Address: _____

_____

City: _____

State: _____ Zip: _____

Ph: _____ Fax: _____

P.O. number (if any): _____	
Number of books:	
Price of book(s) (check below):	
Source code on floppy disk:	$20.00
Plus local sales tax:	
(For CA residents only)	
Plus shipping:	$2.00
(Library/Book rates av.)	
Total amount due:	

Volume discount rates:	Number	Amount
	1-4	$49.95
	5-9	$44.95
	10-19	$39.95
	20-44	$34.95
	45-99	$29.95
	100-above	$24.95